BEING CREATIVE

MICHAEL ATAVAR

BEING CREATIVE

BE INSPIRED.
UNLOCK YOUR
ORIGINALITY.

 WHITE LION
PUBLISHING

Brimming with creative inspiration, how-to projects and
useful information to enrich your everyday life, Quarto
Knows is a favourite destination for those pursuing their
interests and passions. Visit our site and dig deeper with
our books into your area of interest: Quarto Creates,
Quarto Cooks, Quarto Homes, Quarto Lives, Quarto
Drives, Quarto Explores, Quarto Gifts or Quarto Kids.

First published in 2018 by White Lion Publishing
an imprint of The Quarto Group
The Old Brewery, 6 Blundell Street
London N7 9BH
United Kingdom

www.QuartoKnows.com

A catalogue record for this book is available from the British Library.

ISBN 978 1 78131 718 1
Ebook ISBN 978 1 78131 767 9
10 9 8 7 6 5 4 3 2
2022 2021 2020 2019 2018

Designed and illustrated by Stuart Tolley of Transmission Design

Printed in China

CONTENTS

01 BEGINNING

02 USING PROCESS

INTRODUCTION

Welcome.

This book is called *Being Creative*. Note the title 'being' – not 'generating', 'learning' or even 'becoming' creative. These terms imply a journey towards creativity, something that you don't yet own. However, by using the word 'being' I am confirming that you already are creative (you just don't know it).

'Being' is an inner state. It is the generous quality of the child; it is playfulness, exploration and freedom. Whether you accept it or not, whether you activate it or not – you are inherently creative.

Say 'hello' to creativity.

'Being' also implies process, and process is central to this book. Use this volume as a toolkit, a set of procedures that help you, step by step, grow yourself.

Creativity is nothing other than 'you'.

This might be something of a shock. After all, we often treat creativity as if it were a thing separate from us: something that's in the distance, a goal rather than an inner state. It's only glimpsed in the prerogative of other people. I see creativity more as a currency, day-to-day breathing, what's in front of you: not something elevated or obscure, but the everyday seeing of each of us.

This book sets out five major areas: beginning, process, persistence, methodology and ending, each with several active examples. Rather than create a set of rules that you must apply, I've added some experimental formulas, a series of opportunities, and illustrated each section with at least one response from my own practice – a moment when I learned something, got stuck or stepped forward.

I hope that these stories are useful. We often hear that creativity is easy, straightforward, quick to integrate – that's not my experience. I find creativity challenging. However, the creative does hold a lot of potential for personal change and development. It moves you forward dynamically. Through this book you will acquire the abilities and resources needed to find your 'original' self.

I see creativity more as a currency, day-to-day breathing, what's in front of you: not something elevated or obscure, but the everyday seeing of each of us.

A touch of the radical is also useful. There are exercises here that challenge you to be visible, to find your voice. Try to integrate these in small ways. As you descend into an underpass, arrive at a magazine shop or walk along streets filled with discarded wrappers, bring your awareness to these events, locating in each abandoned serviette, each concrete step, a small moment of internal knowledge.

This concentration, this cognition is creativity. It can be achieved anywhere; you can even do it now, as you read this text. It's easy to fool yourself that creative potential lies somewhere else – in computers, in Los Angeles, in superstar vehicles, in Tokyo, in shimmering TV screens. Actually, the contrary is true. It begins with you. The live moment is where creativity happens.

Start with the simple means that you have in front of you now – do not try to abnegate your responsibility by delaying the start. Press play. What is your current reality?

Record it and begin.

HOW TO USE THIS BOOK

This book is organised into five parts and 20 key lessons covering the most current and topical debates of creative thinking today.

Each lesson introduces you to an important concept,

and explains how you can apply what you've learned to everyday life.

As you go through the book, TOOLKITS help you keep track of what you've learned so far.

At BUILD+BECOME we believe in building knowledge that helps you navigate your world. So, dip in, take it step-by-step, or digest it all in one go – however you choose to read this book, enjoy and get thinking.

Specially curated FURTHER LEARNING notes give you a nudge in the right direction for those things that most captured your imagination.

IT BEGINS

WITH YOU.

BEGINNING

LESSONS

My philosophy is that beginning is every day; beginning is life. We are always beginning. Therefore, you can consciously integrate a small amount of beginning into every action, every project.

Here is the first part of the book – it's about beginning.

Simply put: how can you start?

It's easy to become overwhelmed by the fear of beginning. You can get caught up in what you don't have – the perfect studio, the ideal computer, the right job. None of these are present, so you believe that you can't start.

This is usually a defence; perhaps unconsciously you don't really want to begin, so you find fault with the environment and push your anxiety onto that element.

Be careful. Starting is difficult. It demands rigour – it needs direction from you.

However, there are strategies that you can use to overcome this anxiety of starting.

My philosophy is that beginning is every day; beginning is life. We are always beginning. Therefore, you can consciously integrate a small amount of beginning into every action, every project.

In this way, you don't give the feeling of anxiety too much power; you make it a daily action, important, but not overwhelming.

Integrate continuous failure and continuous success into your creativity, so that these elements come to you like waves; they flow through you.

With these methods you can address the fears of beginning while remaining centred, dynamic.

Always, in this book, I will bring the idea back to you. What do you want, think, feel, believe? Therefore, when we look at beginning, we must also discuss what is stopping you from starting.

BEGINNER'S MIND

To help me address the anxiety of starting, I often return to the Zen Buddhist idea of 'beginner's mind' – everything is beginning. You begin every day, every moment. You begin when you breathe, when you inhale and exhale.

In 'beginner's mind' there is possibility, openness, curiosity: all qualities that are useful for an exploration of creativity.

When I remember this simple fact, I return to materiality, to the page. I realise it's just words on the paper – not finished thoughts or polished rhetoric, but simply beginning with what I have with me right now.

We all feel blocked; it's a normal condition of creativity. Everyone feels that they are dealing with difficulty – it's part of the to and fro of being creative.

If you are stuck with your creativity, try the following exercise, which translates Zen 'beginner's mind' into something physical.

+ THE EXERCISE

Take a deep breath.

As you exhale, write on the page, not in a fixed way, but attempting to be uncontrolled, fluid. Note down words: adjectives, colours, feelings. Write until you reach the point when you need to take an in breath.

Then look back – what did you discover?

Don't worry if you can't make sense of what you have written (this is often our fear; that it has to be something straightaway).

The main thing is that you have begun. Congratulations.

Why does this exercise work?

It succeeds because it limits your output to something small and achievable – your breath. It doesn't overwhelm you with too much material; it is eminently do-able.

This is an important part of beginning – sometimes we don't succeed because we begin with an agenda that is too vast, too enormous. The scale of the project is too big.

Therefore, I suggest that you make something small, using the obvious facts of what is close to you:

> **The view from a window**
> **Your shadow**
> **A mark on a wall**
> **The dimensions of a room**

Use anything that's around.

You start by noticing.

In my philosophy, noticing and creativity are synonymous.

When you separate from your creativity, by making it about something other than your seeing, you give the responsibility to someone else. Your act of noticing takes the control and brings the potential for being creative back to yourself.

I was recently in Dublin, preparing for a talk the next day. In the evening, I wandered around the busy city. In one open space, a sandy park, I found some blue bottle tops, lids from plastic water containers of different sizes.

The action I engaged in, this collecting, was a form of beginning.

I took the items and put them in my hotel room, on the table, one after another, reminding me of water, improvisation, fluidity, engagement.

So, when in this book I talk about beginning, I mean the smallest of conscious actions — a performance of self, an experiment that involves you.

Find your own natural level.

MINOR ITEMS

Does this mean that our creative work has no ambition, no scale? Am I suggesting that in essence you do 'nothing'?

Not really.

The big fear that holds us in such thrall is that creative work has to be immediately important. However, in my world of creativity, I want you to think about the opposite. Consider starting small, with minor items; not worrying too much about what things mean; just doing; making things rapidly without any immediate sense of value.

Sometimes it's our delivery-obsessed world that looks at creativity as a series of outcomes that must be achieved. Again, I take a different approach. I think about creativity as a process, a long line of work, that is continuous. Big, small, minor, important. It doesn't matter.

Every so often, we can capture something of this line, make an output, a bundle of what's been happening, to offer to others (a show, a product, an event, a document).

But the line continues onward.

An example of this in action is my own notepad that I carry around with me all the time. It's not full of finished observations, fine-tuned ideas that sit well on the page. It contains:

Drafts ☐

Scribbles ☐

Phone numbers ☐

Dotted lines ☐

A sticking plaster ☐

Circled words ☐

Expenses ☐

It is a series of small, unrelated actions that record my seeing of the world. Each one is distinct, discrete.

Over time, perhaps these events will form something bigger. But for the moment, they are just pieces.

In my notepad I am beginning each time I write on the page; I am actively practising a version of Zen's 'beginner's mind'.

Consider starting small, with
minor items; not worrying
too much about what things
mean; just doing; making things
rapidly without any immediate
sense of value.

+1 212.539.2521

+1 114.162.1725 +1 133.199.1673

REDUCE THE FRAME

A useful feature of beginning is that you can start anywhere: portable you. Since you have beginner's mind, you can see things with fresh eyes — parts that more accomplished viewers might not notice.

You can look at:

> **A car**
> **A flyover**
> **A window**
> **A cloud**

See an object for what it is, simple in its own direct quality, separate from its habit formulas (what it becomes with overfamiliarity).

Remember, you are making as you are breathing, not worrying about what it is or what others think. You are just making 'notes'.

One way to capitalise on this skill that you have just discovered is to record your observations in a notepad. These pages then become the repository of your new, emerging expertise.

Inside the pages, you can grow.

It's often surprising to observe that most people don't record what they notice; they rely on their memory (that imperfect vehicle) to remember what thoughts they have had. Like dreams, ideas drain away and evaporate in the light of day.

A notepad keeps them in one place: discrete, private, emboldened. It says, 'I'm dedicated to creativity; I am taking it seriously.'

Notepads are the engines of creativity. They make things happen.

If we think about creating a rule for creativity — creativity = doing — then notepads are a way of achieving this.

They activate.

+ THE EXERCISE

Go out straightaway and buy a cheap notepad and pen. Don't worry about the quality; in fact, the cheaper the better since you will not worry about making mistakes, crossing out, messiness or unformed ideas.

Carry it with you all the time and write down what you see.

Use the breathing exercise from the previous section to make flurries of words, small sentences. These don't need to be 'about anything'; they can merely be reflections, feelings and observations.

Write them all down.

SUBMARINE ORANGES

It's amazing how little you need to have an idea.

I often work in business contexts teaching people new ways of having ideas, techniques that can provoke their creativity.

When I meet groups for the first time, I often ask them to do very small check-ins:

> Choose a colour
> Name an experience
> Write a key word

Sometimes participants are sceptical of this approach. I tell them, 'This is how artists work', but they don't believe me. Yet when the individuals begin to piece these small elements together, when they put a colour next to a chosen word, they suddenly see an arc, a narrative that they hadn't noticed before.

Everything makes sense.

A good example of this occurred recently in a live context when I was talking to a group of visual artists. Each of them was looking for new ideas to stimulate their practice. When I asked for feedback, one man rapidly listed some of the ideas on his page. The collisions that occurred were startling.

I stopped him at 'Submarine oranges', a run-on of two separate lines that he had written as part of a list. I pointed out what a good title it was. Could he use that?

I reflected to him what he had actually said but not paid attention to: 'Submarine oranges'.

Notepads are a way of noticing these things; they make ideas visible so you can 'see' for the first time. You notice your own 'Submarine oranges' and think: 'Yes, that is a good title. Time to expand.'

+ THE EXERCISE

I'd like to give you a way of working with notepads, to get you started. This method is cheap and simple. Instead of only filling A4 pages, reduce the size to A6. The canvas is therefore smaller, enabling fewer words to be used. Simply fill a page each day, one A6 sheet, 50 words maximum. Not only is this easier, it will give you a sense of achievement, with small steps delivered every day.

Also, extend the idea of 'reducing the frame' in other ways. Write 'small things' in your small A6 notepad. Insignificant observations, minor events.

Keep the idea of 'you' central to these writings; view events with your own eyes.

A4

A6

A5

NOTEPADS
ENGINES O
CREATIVIT
MAKE THIN

ARE THE

F

Y. THEY

GS HAPPEN.

IDEA MUTATES

One further consideration to take into account is that if you don't begin, your idea will never change. It will stick in your head and not develop.

The fact that it changes is positive.

As soon as we start, something alters. The cast-iron conviction that we begin with softens. The mood shifts and we take on the possibility of new information:

> Physicality
> Other people
> Money
> Limitations

You turn towards what is real, actual.

Without this, the idea never develops further than a line on paper.

Therefore, we have to begin both to grow the idea, and to develop ourselves. If we stay in one place, alone with our concept, we will have no challenge and so no possibility for personal growth.

This is important.

Last year, I committed to a period of recording my own dreams. I succeeded in doing this for six months. It was not a theoretical position, an idea on paper, but a piece of process that was physically arduous and difficult to achieve.

I would wake myself up in the night and record what was happening.

At the end of the six-month period, I stopped. However, several weeks later, still tuned in to my own night-time reveries, I dreamt of a project 'ESPELIDES', complete with title. Next day I wrote the idea down and committed to make it.

Without activating the physical research for this piece, via those night-time recordings, I don't think I would have dreamt up my 'ESPELIDES' project. It provided a physical seedbed for the idea, a kind of ferment where it might appear.

My commitment to dreams, the regular loop of recording, allowed me to give up control – once I was in that space of process, it was inevitable that a new idea would naturally emerge.

01	02	03	04	05	06	07	08	09	10
11	12	13	14	15	16	17	18	19	20
21	22	23	24	25	26	27	28	29	30
31	32	33	34	35	36	37	38	39	40
41	42	43	44	45	46	47	48	49	50
51	52	53	54	55	56	57	58	59	60
61	62	63	64	65	66	67	68	69	70
						77	78	79	80
						87	88	89	90
						97	98	99	100

✛ THE EXERCISE

Think about a making a daily commitment of beginning. 1, 5, 10, 50, 100 words every day. The regularity is important. Try and pick a time of day when you do your writing and keep to it:

> Before breakfast
> On the train
> Waiting in a queue
> After hours

The consistency will galvanise you.

YELLOW MOTORBIKE

I have used the word 'mutates' in the title of this section because I enjoy the idea that creative ideas emerge out of mutation – life jumping from one form to another, like the leaps in DNA.

This is often the way that I work with creativity: random words and connections sparking future possibilities. Creativity rarely comes out of organisation, but breeds freely in the petri dish of chaos, fission and error.

+ THE EXERCISE

Try this out in your notebook. Cluster a series of words together (any selection of seemingly random nouns and adjectives).

Choose four to work with in a more concentrated way.

Force a connection with these words.

Push them into a narrative, a feeling, a mosaic, a dialogue.

For example, if the words are:

> Motorbike
> Yellow
> Occidental
> Fashion

How can you corral these words into a relationship? A yellow motorbike appears on the catwalk in London?

If so, what might it be delivering?

A new product, a way of communicating, an idea, a different language?

The motorbike revs up these thoughts.

Very few of my own ideas emerge from my notepad as a fully formed concept.

This is important. Most creatives are working with the smallest pieces of a mosaic, tiny elements that coalesce into more developed structures.

Don't be afraid of the minuscule – this is where all seed ideas grow. Think about pieces, small elements of DNA that mutate, develop over time, like organic plant material. This is not the creativity of must-do or rigidity, stable deliverables, but of play, can-do, accident.

I was recently watching the 1970s film *Rollerball* and noticed that the teams that lit up the neon sign on the score board looked like product titles:

> HOU MAD
> HOU NY
> HOU TOK

Something clicked in my consciousness and I thought, 'Good idea'.

FLIGHT	TIME	DESTINATION
VQ 326	05:34	AMSTERDAM
EP 326	05:45	PARIS
RS 326	06:05	BARCELONA
BA 326	06:20	TOKYO
IQ 326	06:40	NEW YORK
JV 326	07:00	LONDON

+ THE EXERCISE

Look out for odd mixtures of words, wherever you might find them easily:

> Train notice boards
> Till receipts
> Newspaper headlines
> Road signs

See if you can find any unusual alignments. Use them as titles, ways of working, clickable lines of DNA code.

The accidental takes you beyond cliché, beyond the obvious. As you travel on the train home from work, pull in several found elements from your immediate environment; a word, numbers, a headline, colours. Collate them in your mind – what are they all saying?

FAILS, SUCCESSES

All projects begin by trying to activate a thought or an idea into form and substance. The difficulty of that act, of moving them forward into the real, is part of the process. In fact, it's really the whole story.

If we don't begin, it's because we often fear the difficulty. We all fear difficulty (it's natural).

That doesn't mean that we can't deal with it by reducing it to smaller parts – bits and pieces that are more manageable.

Beginning means staying with difficulty. It means that we don't push the difficulty away, we don't put it off until tomorrow.

We stay with it now – with all the terror that it induces.

Of course, as soon as we do this, the difficulty evaporates. It's as if it was never there. When we put pen to paper, it stops. Yet we can keep ourselves in this place of not beginning, a place of fear, for years.

Imagine what that costs us, the investment in not doing.

+ THE EXERCISE

Instead of not beginning, stay with the feeling for 10 seconds.

Breathe deeply; feel the blockage.

Does anything come through: an image, a colour, a sensation?

Stay with the feeling as long as you can, then write it down, describing it in as much detail as possible.

Here, in this hinterland of self, you will find the answers to your challenges.

All projects begin by trying to activate a thought or an idea into form and substance. The difficulty of that act, of moving them forward into the real, is part of the process. In fact, it's really the whole story.

THE WAVES

In our contemporary world we want answers now; we want to begin right away, with success coming fast on its heels.

However, I note that 'beginning' sometimes lasts a long time. In fact, it can take several years. If you want to develop a vocabulary, build a style, invest in a process, create an attitude – sometimes these forms can take some considerable time to grow.

Be patient.

In my own history, my twenties were a period of experiment (fails, successes), with very little obvious output. However, during this time I was learning a lot: how to work with minimal input from others, how to develop DIY projects – I was forced to generate my own ideas from the pieces I found around me.

A good example of this individual approach is my own use of frames.

When I was starting out, I used cardboard coffee-cup holders from a well-known fast-food outlet as frames to hold my cut-up images. At this time, the chain willingly gave out these items free with a small purchase. So I amassed a large amount of these objects.

The down-to-earth qualities of these coffee carriers, coupled with my esoteric images, had a certain charm: a *Threepenny Opera* kind of mischief.

It was only later that I found a form that held all these ideas inside.

So be compassionate, considerate towards yourself. As long as you are working with process (see Part Two), you will be alright.

Remember, the true artist makes their whole life the experiment.

THE EXERCISE

Here is a way of making beginning less arduous and more rewarding.

Divide your project into 100 small parts: a character, a description, a feeling, a scene. Each time, record only that element. Don't worry about the bigger picture.

Stick these smaller parts on your wall, in your A6 notepad format, until all your space has been filled. Once you have assembled these portions, you can work on structure. In the first instance, however, simply develop mood. Step into the work, the visual image, rather than staying outside it.

All creativity is about failure. There's nothing about this experiment that is not concerned with failure. Of course, these fails are small, unnoticed by the general public – they only see the showy outputs of a book release or an exhibition. The day-to-day difficulty is only witnessed by you.

Most of creativity is concerned with the small failures or successes that come every day. Not terrible collapses but simple everyday advancements. I feel that these results are like waves. Sometimes they are enormous, towering, and sometimes they lull you into sleep.

Writing

500 words at a time

Some words scribbled out

A drawing a day

Steps forward

It's possible that this life of waves can also be present in one session, one day.

So if you are working on a project, be aware that your heightened feelings of failure, or success, can be felt in each 24 hours. You might experience each in quick succession.

It's normal.

Personally, I like to think of the day's work as a small, minuscule echo of my entire career. In each 24 hours, I can find joy, lack of inspiration, boredom and success.

This keeps my feet on the ground.

Whatever I am going through – revelations, sticky patches, slow days, jubilation – is exactly as it should be.

TOOLKIT

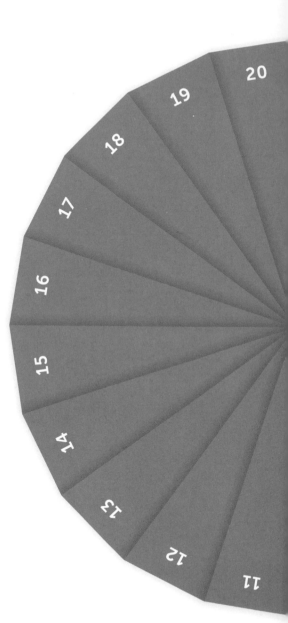

01

Beginning is every day – you are beginning with every page, each project.

That doesn't always mean fear; beginning can also be curiosity, enterprise, play or anticipation.

Beginning is also a quality inside you, malleable, plastic – use what's around you, on the street, to activate this feeling. In this way, you won't feel alone. Beginning is objects, is everything, is the world.

02

You don't need a lot of material to have an idea – it's more your manipulation of small processes that will lead to revelation. Emblematic of this approach is the A6 page, a reduced format that encourages you to write, to create.

Step into this page, as if through a new window.

Noticing is an active key; once you see what's around you, once you become aware, you can consciously step forward into the creative.

03

Creativity = doing.

Action is the only way to move into something new. If you don't physicalise an idea, it will never change. You will remain in the conceptual, only staying with graph paper ideas.

A commitment to doing will provoke a change in your creative process. If you record the incidental, the passing flux with real enthusiasm, you will place yourself right in the vortex of creativity.

04

Action necessarily involves experiment. That can provoke failure, but don't worry — failure and success are normal components of creative life. There is no creativity without appropriate failure.

The normal process of every 24 hours contains the explicit language of being creative — success, boredom, wrong turns, mistakes, minor triumphs.

Creativity often feels like a cul-de-sac. Keep going.

FURTHER LEARNING

READ

Crooked Cucumber: The Life and Teaching of Shunryu Suzuki
David Chadwick (Broadway Books, 1999)

Rollerball Murder
William Harrison (Futura Publishing, 1975)

ABC of Reading Ezra Pound
(New Directions Paperbook, 1960)

The Daily Practice of Painting: Writings and Interviews 1962–1993
Gerhard Richter (Thames & Hudson, 1995)

Not Always So: Practicing the True Spirit of Zen
Shunryu Suzuki (HarperCollins, 2002)

LISTEN

Shunryu Suzuki
Suzuki's talks from the Tassajara Zen Mountain Center cover a variety of subjects – birds, objective self, the present, sound and noise, the other. These lectures are widely available in film format online and indicate a complex philosophy of now, simply and elegantly expressed.

STUDY

Counselling and psychotherapy training
The Gestalt Centre, London, UK

Mindfulness
Centre for Mindfulness, Amsterdam, The Netherlands

The School of Life
Alain de Botton's The School of Life offers many different courses in self-development and business intelligence. Choose one of its evening classes available at a variety of European schools.

VISIT

Rhodia
I favour the Rhodia brand of notepads, A5 black cover with blue squared pages inside. However, don't obsess about acquiring the same edition. Visit your local newsagent or supermarket to buy a notepad and paper. Any cheap shorthand pad will do. I buy books on the move – in airports, foreign shops, cash and carry retailers. The more expensive the brand, the less likely you are to write in it.

USING PROCESS

LESSONS

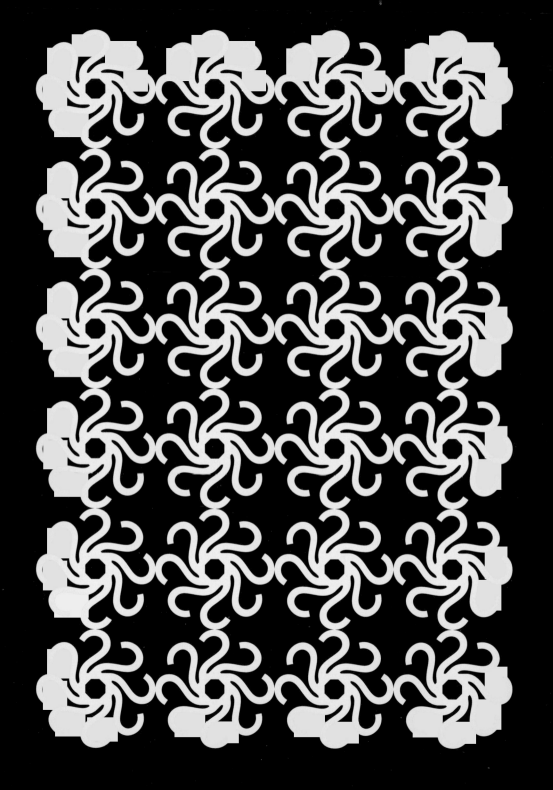

Don't be afraid of yourself. Your flaws, your imperfect eye, are actually your greatest assets — because they make what you see quite different from everyone else.

Here is the second part of the book — it's about process.

A basic question: what do you already have?

Sometimes you think that you have nothing, that there are few resources available, but process helps you to interrogate the blank page — it shows you that even in that seeming nothingness there is content, there is life.

In fact, the white empty page is a deep resource; it's a mirror reflecting back yourself.

Process is a tool that helps you question what's really happening, mapping what you see onto the page. It doesn't engage in the fantasies of what creativity might be, it doesn't rely on fortune-telling, but it works with what is present, what is seen.

Piece by piece, using a mirror reflection of self, you transfer what you see in the world onto the page.

Don't be afraid of yourself.

Your flaws, your imperfect eye, are actually your greatest assets — because they make what you see quite different from everyone else. We tend to fear this individuality. I hope to show you that there's nothing fearful about idiosyncratic seeing. In fact, it's the basis of all creativity.

Be alive to phenomena — it's the only method I know for stimulating the creative impulse. Branches, dirt, train tracks, floating rubbish; make these your friends in the search for new ideas, fresh design.

Don't worry about sophisticated tools. If you have yourself on board, you will be fine.

SMALL WORD PROCESS

Optimistic

Curious

Process is what is happening inside you right now, whether you are:

Curious ☐

Negative ☐

Enthusiastic ☐

Bored ☐

Optimistic ☐

Sensitive ☐

Open ☐

Undecided ☐

This moment of now is always the best material for activating the creative impulse. If you wander away from that, if you fantasise about other realities, the energy tends to dissipate.

Take three pieces of paper and write on each one simple word.

What best describes where you are right now?

Don't think too much about the question. Quickly write down the first three words that come to mind. Note if they are active or receiving, if they assemble into a mood or disconnect from each other, if they are thinking or feeling.

Quickly write down these further impressions – you have now entered the world of process.

Why is this exercise important?

It's useful because it brings the debate about creativity back to you:

> **What you see**
> **What you feel**
> **What you hear**

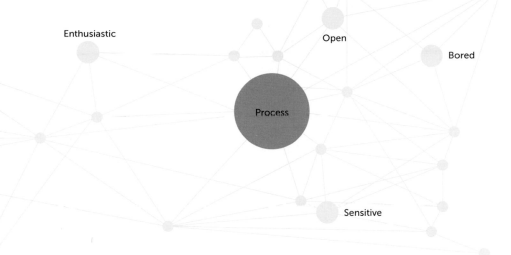

All creativity is simply mapping these internal ideas and emotions onto the page.

Creativity is not an independent force, separate from you. It 'is' you, with all the challenges and difficulties that your daily creativity presents.

Therefore when you notice a cloud, see a piece of dust on the pavement, recognise happiness, hold up a coffee cup, note a reflection of a balloon or recall a series of colours, you are also activating process; it's another version of the 'three words' exercise. All these observations are material for your creativity. Recording these ideas allows you to remain in touch with yourself. It also makes you conscious of what was previously unseen, unconscious.

Since creativity is awareness of what is around you, the action of saving these observations in your notepad renders them real, authentic.

It pins them to the page.

It's important to look at what's right in front of you.

Recently I was teaching in Madrid. When I came out of the workshop space, I walked towards the underground and noticed that the pavement was full of fallen seeds. I thought: we don't need to travel to Mars to find novelty, because Mars is here in everything, inside us, everywhere we look — in the dust, on the pavement, in the sunset.

On the train I immediately wrote in my notepad a reminder of this universal feeling:

> The temporary
> Use anything
> Pull it towards you
> Begin now

CHAOS THAT COUNTS

One simple way I have found of developing process is to write lists.

These strings of words, vertical on the page, are pieces of elastic that stretch from you, pulling out experience, words and images.

You can make these lists rapidly, automatically, not thinking too deeply about them. They are like versions of thrown dice, puzzles, chance procedures – by accident telling you something about what is inside you.

These lists could be titles, instructions, names or methods.

The following example is taken from my current notepad:

> Slowly ... **light comes**
> **The whole**
> **Step number one**
> **Hands**
> **Blank (what do you wish for?)**
> **Acceptance**

It illustrates how unintegrated these lists can be. Process is irrational, contrary – it works by accumulating material every day, through the action of self-collecting. Remember, you are not searching for newness, or referencing the exotic, you are simply noting in detail the everyday materials that are around you.

Most of it will never find any final form, and that's the point. It's process, moving things forward. However, once you start to record it, you find, surprisingly, that you already have a version of creativity.

It's yours alone.

Process also teaches you that everything is interesting, if you stay with it.

Then you will discover that even the most banal piece of nothing will have conceptual and formal conceits that can be used in your own creativity.

I'm always surprised how much can be accumulated from unassuming material. In fact, that's where I tend to look.

When I was making my solo show 'Dusk' (2006), I deliberately went to abandoned places to record the changes in light levels at twilight. Running the camera over time, waiting, I also made a recording of myself, my feelings, while I remained there watching.

This is creativity as pure process — mapping what is inside.

Often I think that there's nothing other than this; we pretend that it's about something else, but it's not about anything other than our emotions.

When I look back at the recordings of 'Dusk', as I watch them pulse, I am also seeing my own heartbeat.

These void spaces, in the city, are the perfect place to explore process in a deep and profound way.

Lastly, it's important to record.

It's easy to forget this, to abandon doing and retreat to a mental space of creativity, staying in the abstract.

Sadly, this never works.

It's the lightning-flash recording of the pen on paper, wayward, unpredictable, improvisatory, where thing happen.

Process leads you from any direction to the right idea. You might have many thoughts that don't eventually work out (that's normal). But still, by doing them, activating these avenues, you create a preparedness for the right idea to finally appear.

This can't be underestimated.

Process happens when it's live on paper, not recollected in tranquillity.

It's the chaos that counts.

INTERNAL CAMERA

A major feature of process is that you turn the view, away from the external world towards yourself. You don't blank out what's there; rather you bring awareness to yourself, and with that focus in place, you see the outside world with new eyes.

In fact, because you pay attention to yourself, and are more curious, you relate more accurately to what's around you.

I call this process 'internal camera'.

When you are blocked, in your mind's eye try turning the camera towards you, recording what's going on inside.

What do you see? What do you notice?

Simply record with your new 'internal camera'.

Often we are told not to trust what we see, so we leave these images behind in the search for more conventional approaches. But these first, unformed, intuitive recordings are usually the best way of staying in touch with our creativity.

Trust that what your vision rests on is useful and important. This imperfection is yourself in amplified form.

Within this philosophy, intuition, self and creativity are, in fact, all the same word.

So, even if you see:

A tunnel ☐

Used burger wrappers ☐

Broken light fixture ☐

Sunset window ☐

This is process reality for you, and shouldn't be denied. For example, imagine a tunnel takes you down underground, into the unconscious, or a sunset reminds you about possible endings, the end of perception. For every observation, make a simple analogue, a heightened version, tied to the real but allowed to fly further.

In this way, everything becomes the material of your creativity.

So when I talk about your 'camera', I mean any conscious way of seeing that you can trust: cognisant, real, sentient. Allow yourself to record – trust that what you see is the key to unlocking your creativity.

We often don't succeed because we limit our creativity time to when we are supposed to be having ideas – in the boardroom, at our desks, working on projects – the times that we are paid to be creative. This really reduces the space for

Creativity is not about the objective reality of what's actually there, but how you see it, in all your eccentricity and confusion.

creative thinking to a very few short minutes each day.

Ideas happen in a different way – all the time, accidentally, serendipitously: on the street, standing in a queue. They are like breathing, fried onions on a hot-dog stand, exhaust fumes or cigarette smoke blown in your face. They permeate the city 24 hours a day.

Each object and event has its own ephemeral 'double' that rapidly evaporates if not recorded. This 'double' is your seeing of it, the vision, and your distinctive reading of it through your own 'internal camera'.

Of course, most of this is lost, not seen by anyone at all. But every incident is creative fuel for you; it can be recorded in your individual version of creativity.

Try carrying a notepad around with you at all times to record these short-lived 'doubles'.

Don't hesitate to write things down in it; it doesn't matter what the content is.

It could be lists, colours, descriptions, objects, intentions. It could be the recording of the small print on your train ticket – that is your 'double', its rewriting.

It could be anything.

A FRENZY NOONDAY

Working through these 'doubles' is a natural part of creativity. In fact, the copying out by hand of someone else's work, or the pieces that you find on your journeys, is a legitimate practice that can lead you to some interesting results. For example, as a teenager I rewrote passages from J.D. Salinger's *Franny and Zooey* in order to internalise Salinger.

I 'swallowed' J.D. and by an act of transferred magic, took his inspiration into me. You might worry that you don't have an original idea, that everything has been done before, that all avenues are blocked. Don't worry. Simply copy out by hand what you see in front of you. It's a process of transmutation.

The natural mistakes that you create, the accidents of spelling, will turn the 'classic' into something more contemporary, true for you.

'A Frenzy Noonday' (an anagram of 'Franny and Zooey').

I often use these word experiments when working in corporate contexts. The oddity of these small, overturned elements allows the clients to see outside their frame of reference (the business window) — encouraging a piece of play to happen.

Imagine your creative work as a series of flexible arms that reach out beyond you, gathering information.

The experimental allows you to take this approach. Rather than working horizontally and chronologically in a series of strategic moves (from idea, to product, to output), the experimental allows you to take chances. It jump-cuts across space, landing on something unexpected.

Imagine your creative work as a series of flexible arms that reach out beyond you, gathering information – just like those mobile claws that you see in fairground arcades, destined for the fluffy toy, the prize dinosaur, the key ring.

These green monster arms collect the experimental data from you and record it in your notepad, as your prize, avoiding the clichés of what is normally seen.

So whatever you note down, make it intrinsic to you:

> Jumps
> Monster green
> Unique prize
> Flexible clichés
> Claws

It's all a game in which you can continue to play, using process as guide.

CREATIVITY

INDEPENDEN

SEPARATE F

IT 'IS' YOU.

IS NOT AN
T FORCE,
ROM YOU.

SUBVERT HABIT

Some people might regard the individuality that emerges from your 'internal camera' as a mistake. They could say that your photographs are out of focus, or perhaps pointing in the wrong direction, upside down. These critics will look at your notepad and only see scribbles, chaotic recording.

Yet chaos is authentic process; these mistakes are often the basis of creativity.

They are process moments in concentrated form. They take you beyond habit formulas into a place where things can be seen differently.

So ignore other people, and pay attention to the errors when they occur.

In most creativity, we are unconsciously reproducing ideas that we have seen elsewhere — through TV, advertising, films. In fact, 90% of all output is from these areas. These formulas are difficult to shift; they quickly drive a nail into our deep selves.

So when you see something, you are not really seeing, you are looking through the spectacles of culture, the 3D glasses of control. This makes it difficult to approach anything with new eyes.

In an attempt to subvert habit, try the following exercise:

+ THE EXERCISE

At your desk, rotate your chair so that you are turned away from the computer screen. Now check in with your 'internal camera'.

What is the first image that you see?

Concretise this impression, finally, by recording the idea in your notepad.

Well done.

You have turned away from what is forward-facing, correct, prosaic, chronological and have approached the reverse, the inverted, the opposite.

(At least here you have a chance to be original.)

This small physical action, of turning around, can allow you to fast-track to your internal self and so speed up process. In fact, this physical intervention can accelerate creativity by increasing sensitivity and awareness.

I often use these methods, adapted from Gestalt, to speed up change — the physical overruns the mental and briefly quashes the ego, allowing a series of small errors to occur.

Quick ... catch.

BLACK TAPE 'X'S

Physical action also makes you visible, as if you are heading in the reverse path of traffic. By turning your chair to the opposite of the screen, you adopt an attitude that is more exposing.

I recently experienced this on a piece of wasteland in London. I noticed that the windows of a newly constructed block still had some large black tape 'X's stuck to the inside of the glass, making the dusty surface like an enlarged photographic contact sheet, with individual images crossed out.

I made some of my own images of the 'X's, writing down the name and serial number from the side of a silvered piece of breeze block that I found on the pavement, which to me, appeared to have fallen from a recent space mission. Around me, construction staff, on the ground and in their lorries, looked at me oddly.

I felt in the position of the outsider, but understood that my feelings might be important, so I stayed with my uncomfortableness as long as possible, until I could finally move away.

This process reminded me that physically stepping outside the world of habitual reality, can provoke my creativity. This can be achieved on any city street corner, piece of wasteland or traffic island.

You merely have to stop and look.

'But,' you might protest, 'what if I don't have your physical boldness? What if I am embarrassed to show myself?'

Creativity is active, requires bravery, is deliberate. But your writing is the perfect vehicle for any exploration of self. You can play with identity here on the page.

+ THE EXERCISE

Try this exercise to explore the notion of difficulty.

Imagine a series of tests, journeys or environments that might be the opposite of what you are used to:

> **Alien city**
> **Deserted campus**
> **Naturist beach**
> **Forest**
> **Primordial swamp**
> **Airport**
> **Leather bar**
> **B.C.**

Note down whatever feels intolerable to you.

Write some lines about the culture and experience of this place – you will often find that what you record is something closer to home, something alive now. By immersing yourself in what feels wrong, you might find some unlikely allies. For example, if the 'forest' description focuses on your fear of the unknown, pull that element into your work, introducing a portion of chaos, or ineffability, into your creative process.

I like to reel in the opposite, my fears, in this way, making them part of the work: not hidden, but visible, active and seen.

It's like throwing paint at my personality until I surrender.

CRUMBS, IDEAS

There is no part of creativity that is not about looking, paying attention, noticing. So pull into your world view the everyday – the materials that surround you, what arrives on the pavement, the pieces of the world.

Do this first by recording, writing in your notepad.

+ THE EXERCISE

One trick I have for achieving this I call 'assisted seeing', and it goes like this:

Spend one minute recording what you see.

Write continuously.

Keep your eyes glued to what you are recording, ignoring everything else. I find this helps. It doesn't matter if the words are illegible on the page. Simply make the paper an action event, directed by your writing.

The task is not to stop, allowing all mistakes that arrive – these errors can then be folded back into your practice in a coherent way.

This 'assisted seeing' can be extended for 1, 2, 3, 5, 10 minutes, if you can tolerate it.

(If you could imagine doing this every day, you are on your way to making a longer commitment to writing.)

You might think that faced with the blankness of your own experience you would find nothing. Yet, that's not what I have discovered. When you look with your own eyes, you see something in an original way.

Time slows down, the moment grows, everything expands.

I often attempt this exercise when I find myself alone in a café, waiting for someone to arrive. In the few garbled minutes, I record what's happening. It's a form of concentrated looking and has resulted in some of my most personal, intense, solo experiences.

I remember recently sitting in a West End fast-food chain with big windows overlooking the street, observing the church opposite and writing in my notepad, simply noting my own impressions.

(Sometimes I don't bother to look at the paper.)

I recalled the name of the building opposite, 'Church of the Assumption' – and so following my own process, I reflected on the following question: what had I previously assumed to be correct? This is a good example of process in action – I wrote a list of these 'assumed' things, 20 items running down the page in one long ladder.

In this stillness, the flash of the moment, I was inside my own creativity, absorbed in the narrowness of now.

It also shows how several of the actions that you have learnt so far in the book can be combined into one complex activity:

> Lists
> Assisted seeing
> Process
> Internal camera
> Action

When you activate the creative, you are not staying in one domain – you are mutating forms, melting, jumping between experiences, using several skills. It's this crucible, activated physically, that begets creativity.

When you limit yourself to only one area of practice, say 'action', you will be creative only until this reservoir of activity dries up; then you will have no internal process to work with.

Although this sounds an unlikely scenario (how can action ever be wrong?), it's a common problem in business environments.

If you hit a brick wall, and things don't work as before, it's because the barrier represents a challenge to feeling. When you deal with what's inside, the problem usually evaporates.

CURIOUS, OPEN, UNDECIDED

If you feel that you don't have the skills to
attempt these tasks, a short cut to process is to
work with colour.

Colour runs riot through boundaries, pushing
you forward in direct, unconditional ways.

+ THE EXERCISE

Quickly pick three colours from your
immediate environment:

> **High-res orange**
> **Dirty white**
> **Painted wood edge**
> **Yellow dot**
> **Intense, hard red**

(It doesn't matter what you choose.)

Make a narrative cluster from the three
colours: not necessarily a story, more an
impression, a sense of connectivity – a
common feeling that they might all contain.
Finally, pick one colour from the selection,
look at it directly, let it hold your entire field
of vision, close up to your eyes, and absorb it.

Then go back several sections to page
44, and combine your three words from that
exercise with the final colour selected here.

Put the words and the colour physically
on the table.

Perhaps it's the colour choice 'High-res
orange' with the words:

> **'Curious'** ?
> **'Open'**?
> **'Undecided'**?

What do the colour and the words mean to
you?

Is there any journey that you have made
while reading Part Two of this book that is
reflected here in the choices in front of you?
If so, what?

Colour

What do the colour and the
words mean to you?

Using Process

TOOLKIT

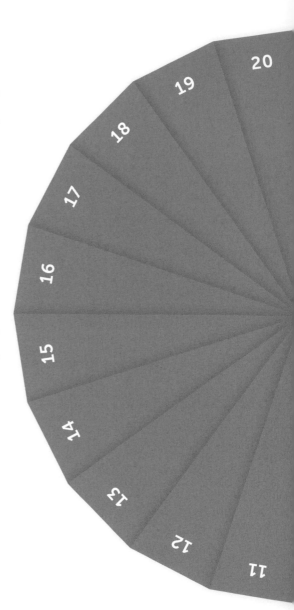

05

Recording is an active part of creative process. Noting things down makes them actual – the ideas don't fly away, instead they stick like glue to the page. What happens in an improvisatory way when you are just playing 'is' creativity.

These fleeting moments, the words created in error, are a necessary part of creativity, so write them down.

You can't be creative without activating your own reality.

06

Creativity is not elsewhere; it is inside you.

What you record with your internal camera – whether eccentric, confusing, difficult or impenetrable – is worth staying with, is valuable. Often we are taught that these observations are not worthy of recording, that we don't have any creativity at all. The opposite is true; the individual always ignites uncommon and exclusive approaches.

That's what you are aiming for – solo vision, irregular and distinctive. Treat your mistakes as a form of outrage against conventional logic.

07

Visibility is often the analogue of process. To record what you see around you, with your internal camera, you will have to cultivate some bravery. However, don't be afraid that you need to make giant steps – the small, slight recording of everyday is a form of courage.

Work with what you don't understand to explore yourself more fully; work with what hasn't been experienced by you before.

08

All the techniques of this book can be used simultaneously to generate a dense process that can provoke creativity.

Lists, assisted seeing, process, internal camera, action: create a bigger cloud of material that overlaps, mixes, abuts, interpenetrates.

Use them as colours, blending into each other; experiment as you would with a palette, moving from one tone to another.

FURTHER LEARNING

READ

A William Burroughs Reader
William S. Burroughs, edited by John Calder
(Pan Books, 1982)

Rub Out The Words: Letters 1959–1974
William S. Burroughs, edited and with an
introduction by Bill Morgan (Penguin Modern
Classics, 2012)

***River's Way: The Process Science of the
Dreambody*** (Arnold Mindell, Routledge
& Kegan Paul, 1985)

For Inspiration Only
Future Systems (John Wiley & Sons, 1996)

Franny and Zooey
J.D. Salinger (Penguin, 1964)

FOLLOW

Black Mountain College
Explore the output of this liberal arts
education centre 1933–1957. The faculty
included, at different times, Josef Albers,
Merce Cunningham, John Cage and
Buckminster Fuller.

STUDY

PHotoEspaña, Madrid, Spain
Sign up for advanced studies or the masters
programme at PHE/PIC.A. PHotoEspaña is
an international festival of visual arts and
photography based in Madrid.

The Photographer's Gallery, London, UK
Take a course in your 'external camera' at
this London gallery. Their current workshops
include explorations of Polaroids, coding for
visual artists, performance and photography.

VISIT

Pret a Manger
Allow your diary to include at least one hour
sitting alone in the window seat of any large
chain of coffee shops. Vary your schedule to
move each week between different outlets.
Sit looking out and record what you see – if
necessary, recycle your paper coffee cup and
use it as a notepad to write on. Let the large
windows be your eyes.

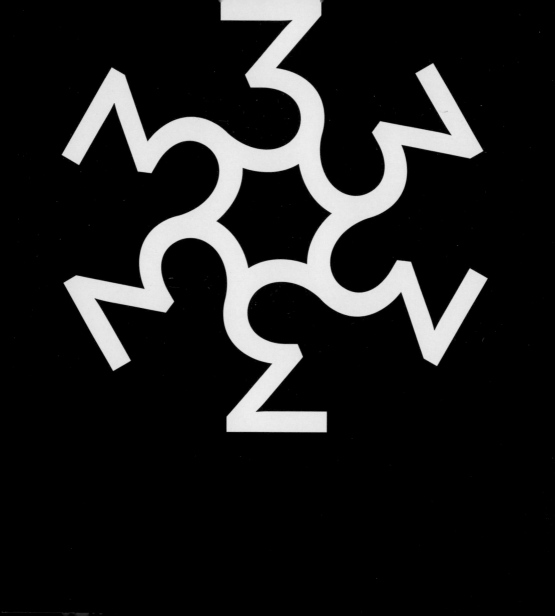

KEEPING GOING

LESSONS

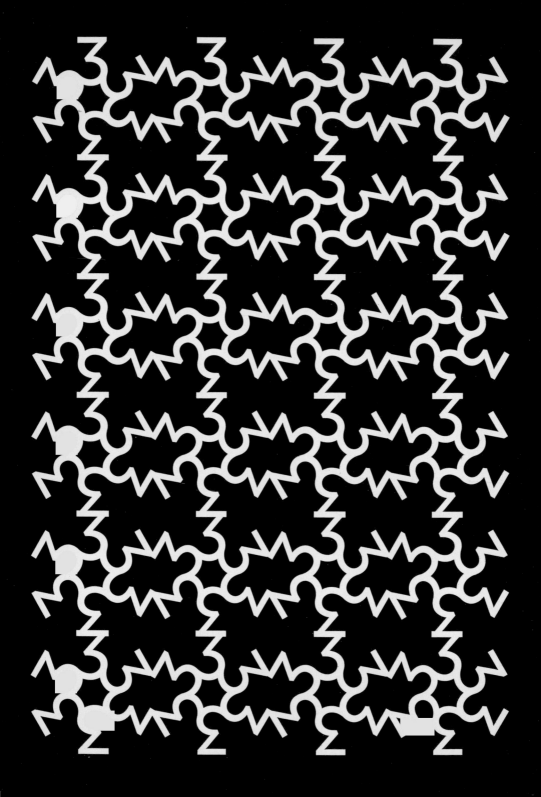

We fantasise about the imperial peaks of writers, creatives, artists, but essentially they are working every day to achieve small, local goals.

Here is the third part of the book – it gives you advice about ways to keep going.

It asks a very simple question: how do I cultivate persistence?

Of course, the beginning – if we can start – is a large step, and the outcome, the product – if we see it at all – is a long way off. What happens in the middle ground, the space where you have to keep turning the material over, each day making something that often feels less than perfect?

How do you keep going during this stretch?

Often you can use the tools that you already have learned about in this book – notepads and process. If you have these two elements, all becomes possible.

Don't worry; you can do it. The key to persistence is small steps every day.

It doesn't need the voluminous attack we imagine all creatives have; instead, what is required are negligible, modular moves, repeated every day.

Record with your 'internal camera' – whatever you can easily manage.

This is the process through which I am writing this book: a small amount of material generated every 24 hours, in my notepad and on the computer.

We fantasise about the imperial peaks of writers, creatives, artists, but essentially they are working every day to achieve small, local goals.

They are not idols, but people who also drive cars, put the rubbish out, go to the supermarket and watch TV.

They are people just like you.

PERSISTENCE

If I want to persist, to keep going, I reduce the scale of my attention to something very small. I occupy the narrow space of now. This tight confine pushes me forward into creativity, without making its demands too difficult.

The classic, narrow window of attention is 10 minutes.

Here, contemplation can be focused in a precise, direct way (like a sharpened pencil), on what is in front of you.

Let's try it now in your notepad – for 10 minutes record anything that you like.

This could be words, doodles, lists, sketches, lines. Try and fill the whole time with writing, without thinking of what you are doing. I often find that the blankness of the empty mind – not considering, just doing – is the thing that moves me forward.

Abandon your critical self for just a few short minutes at a time.

Put this censuring mind in the waste bin.

Unfortunately, there is no super-theory that can conceptualise creativity for you and make the practice of 'doing it' go away, or allow you to eradicate this arduous step of actually making the work.

(I've tried, believe me.)

Creativity is a practice that involves doing. Pen on paper, brush in ink, the physical reminds you of where you are, your place in the world and what you need to do.

However, these 10 minutes of 'noticing', narrowed like lightning onto the tip of your felt-tip, provide persistence by pushing you quickly forward through the barriers of inertia, towards something made:

A page

A title

An observation

A study

These can be strung together to create modular forms that are complex, distinct.

These 10 minutes remind me of the cord and rice-paper zigzag sculptures that you find outside Shinto shrines in Japan — like mini lightning flashes advising you to pay attention to what is in front of you.

Just like the materials I'm suggesting in this book, they are made of simple paper and cord, nothing special. However, assembled in long strings, occupying space, they have a big impact — they welcome you into the space. Anything is possible here.

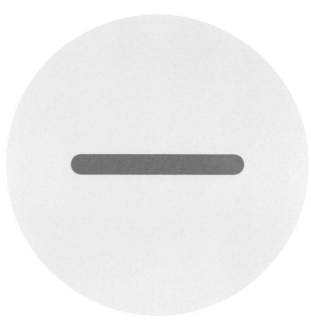

SHIFT AND BLUR

You might be thinking, doesn't this just result in a series of diary entries that are personal, autobiographical, of use to no one else?

That's true — they start off like that, because often you don't know what you are doing. You start believing one thing to be true, but after a few days the fantasies about your creativity burn off. Something gets exposed. Then you reach a different level, a rich centre, that might be about something quite different.

Your external view becomes internal.

If you can continue the exercise for 30 days, I guarantee that you will find yourself in a completely different territory.

Your view will be allowed to shift and blur, moving from one state to another.

Here's one further tip: when you write, collect, or draw for 30 days, don't look back. Hide the paper away in a folder, or turn over the pages of your notepad. You will be tempted to review, but resist. Only reveal the contents after the 30 days are up.

Again, in this way, you limit your critical self and push forward towards the new, raw core of something else.

Be patient.

You will often find that your creativity only presents itself to you as a problem, an issue of persistence, when you think about the possible future of your work, the eventual output.

If you worry what comes 'after' creativity (exhibition, book, recording) you will start to stress.

It reminds me of when I was on a residency on Itaparica, off the coast of Salvador, in Brazil. One evening, I picked up a bike taxi to the port on the other side of the island — I sat on the back of the

Be patient. You will often find that your creativity only presents itself to you as a problem, an issue of persistence, when you think about the possible future of your work, the eventual output.

motorbike wearing shorts and a light shirt, my arms around the driver. As we came to the top of the mountain, right in the centre, surrounded by palm trees, the rain started to pour down. It was like a caesura, one side sunny, the other in cloud and rain, with me in the middle, soaking wet.

I reflected on the mindset that sees one part as negative, the other as positive.

Here I was, deep in process, riding the line between the two.

And I realised that when I am truly in the moment, there is no good and bad – only events. When I don't worry about the future of my writing, when I don't stress about 'after' but just do it, then I can be truly creative.

If you don't theorise about creativity, or overthink it, you achieve more.

Just do.

RECORD EVERY DAY

My insistence on 30 days is an important factor.

Thirty days is the minimum amount of process needed to allow a shift of emphasis to occur – time is an important factor in allowing change to happen.

It's compelling to believe that all this creativity can be accomplished on page one, but it's impossible. No one can start on the blank page and write a masterpiece. Masterpieces are only accumulations of detail.

However, you must begin by recording one individual example.

I've tackled this challenge by setting myself tasks, long-term strings of small exercises that stretch over days and months – successive accumulations of 24-hour periods that loop and twist in final, completed formats. For example, in my own recent 'A-B' dialogue with artist Roelof Bakker, we managed 158 consecutive posts between the two of us – a conversation that extended over a two-year stretch; practising autobiography, chains of self.

I'm not suggesting that you dive into a long, challenging series (be careful of taking on too much).

However, how about: every hour for a day, 7 days, one photograph every 24 hours, 10 quiet minutes repeated, 30 days.

Take yourself just beyond the limit of what feels do-able, into the blue extent of what might be.

Also, see if you can organise it each time to occupy the same hour and space:

Canteen – 10am ☐

Park – 1pm ☐

Underground train – 5pm ☐

Pizza restaurant – 7pm ☐

Hotel – 9pm ☐

Bed – 2am ☐

If you position yourself in strict circumstances 'to receive', like an antenna catching data, eventually you will net something. Even if your mind roams, in your repeated action you will be physically concentrated, here in the space of waiting for ideas.

In these brief 10 minutes each day, you can switch from the bigger narrative, the must-dos of creativity, the ambition of the larger impetus, and just return to activating.

30

PARKING A CAR

Repetition is useful as it allows you to relax into making.

You don't begin again each day; you repeat an action that was pre-selected, slotting a new text or image into the vacant space, just like parking a car.

The value of this practice is to reduce anxiety – if you are simply making, you can work on automatic, just seeing and switching off any critical perspectives.

Repetition makes this possible.

If I arrive at my desk every day at 9am, as close to the time of waking as possible, to dreams, in order to stimulate the unconscious, and work each morning, until lunch, I provide this accommodated 'parking space' for myself simply to get on with things.

I therefore have a practice that is just about doing.

This idea of persistence supported by individual moments in 30-, 60-, 90-day strings is a practice – the daily rehearsal of small moments that accumulate dexterity and expertise. After all, what is a novel but 32,850 singular moments (30 minutes each day x 3 years) slotted into a larger format?

My own background in performance art, allows me to think of these daily rituals, these 90-day strings of experiences as actions that move the pieces forward. Nothing might be happening, but by:

Parking the car ☐

Filing papers ☐

Cleaning a window ☐

Buying a ticket ☐

Washing the floor ☐

each day, at the same time, a complex trajectory forms.

These actions from the avant-garde of the 1970s have now become part of popular creativity – take a photo every day, document your every meal, collect your rubbish.

George Brecht, Tehching Hsieh and Dieter Roth – it would be a good idea to emulate the practice of these artists. They remind us that process is valuable – what we previously thought of as the background material, the research, is actually also the art.

Any action, however small, repeated continuously for longer than five minutes, will take you out of yourself into a larger space, beyond the body.

Where I am sitting now, I try a repeated action; if I sit down and stand up for one minute, practising at my desk, I step into a new version of me, a 'not-me', that can allow transformation to happen.

(Be careful to practise these systems only within your own personal limits.)

Through repetition, you explore a bigger self, the world of the artist – one that you have always been waiting for.

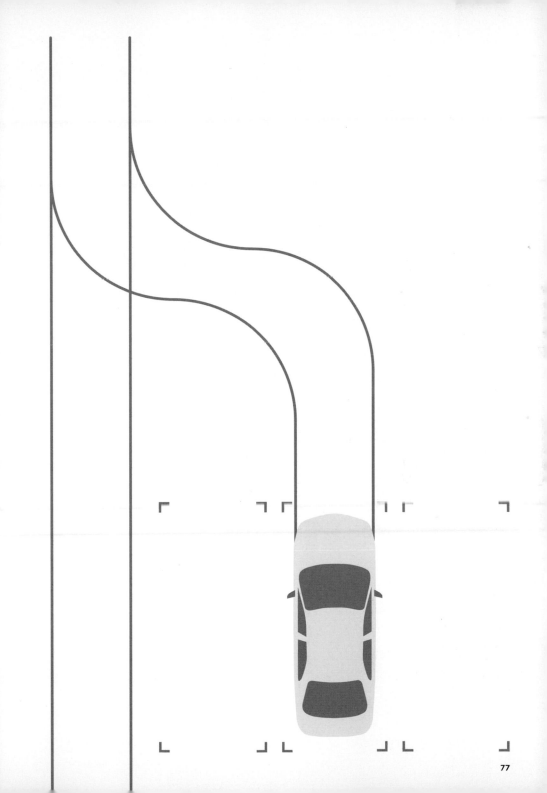

PROCESS M
BY RECORDI
COMPLEXITY
STEPS, EVE

ULTIPLIED
NG EQUALS
. SMALL
RY DAY.

INSIDE JOURNEYS

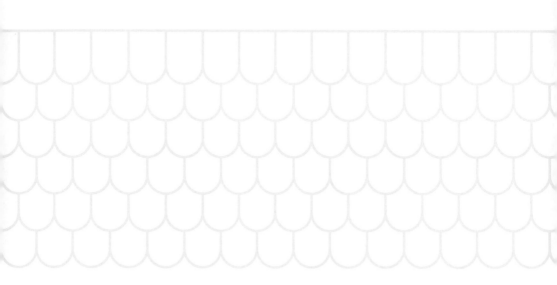

However, what happens if you fail after several days to write in your notepad, if you falter?

I often find that the idea of the journey can help. It takes you out of the mental confines of your desk, which narrows your potential by only working when facing your computer screen, and offers you some kindness, a quality that is quite underrated in your creativity work.

You step out of habit formulas and collide with the real world of events.

In this new space, a bird, a car horn blaring, or the number five on a dial, jumps out at you. These events can offer you unexpected solutions to difficult creative challenges by disturbing your fixed idea of reality (intractable in your head), and supplanting it with another, better version.

Perhaps this underlying theme of kindness is intimately connected with 'inside journeys'.

The journey allows the warm qualities of exploration to penetrate the tough core of relentless work. Be kind to yourself — these adventurous journeys away from your desk can often offer solutions that are quite unexpected.

Strategic journeys can revive you. Try this technique. Enact a small journey:

> **Walk to the shops**
> **Take a lift to the top floor**
> **Circle the block**
> **Pick up a bus for one stop**

(Keep it simple to begin with.)

These journeys are an 'ideas ambush'.

Strategic journeys can revive you.

In the first few days of being in a foreign city, you will experience an agreeable dislocation that allows you to see without your cultural blinkers on.

I accentuate this by travelling without a map or guidebook. However, this narrow window of freedom is brief, it closes quickly; so remember that when you look with new eyes at a pile of lemons, building materials, or a battered red car, these original views are short-lived.

Record them rapidly in your notepad.

Arriving on a Sunday in Madrid, I felt the visibility that only being alone in a foreign place can give you. I chased the sun as it dropped beyond the station at Atotcha, knowing that this short phase of

the sun would soon be over and with it my embarrassment and originality would be lost. So I sat outside with the skateboarders, writing in my notepad and watching the locals take selfies until the light faded.

These games of inside and out, a kind of hide-and-seek with yourself, are useful elements of 'inside journeys'; they take you beyond the physical confines of office and home into a more exposed version of reality.

You can't rely on the set formula, the routine approach. Instead, you feel lost, abandoned, in a strange place. This game of hide-and-seek that I describe here is a way of stepping into vulnerability and difficulty in order to stimulate process

Strategic journeys can force us to deal with reality in a new way.

BURST BALLOON

These strategies from this section of the book – repetition, 10 minutes, inside journeys, 30 days, regularity – offer you a lifeline that pulls you forward to the future.

They are the now that is repeated over and over.

It reminds me that your own 'journey' extends into the future, beyond the moment of making, creating a virtual interior landscape that is continuous.

You are never limited by now.

The ironic fact is that by focusing on 10 minutes, on the now, you expand your potential and creative consciousness beyond what's happening right in front of you into a bigger space of self. This might seem impossible – but try it and see. I guarantee that your virtual interior landscape will expand.

Think of it as putting on a VR headset; suddenly your attention bristles, your awareness is optimum, you can see clearly.

I've often taken the idea of journeys to extreme levels, making solo trips actively to generate projects – I travelled to Taiwan and Japan to create my work '[four walls]' (2004). On the way I way I reflected on barking dogs, the Confucius Temple, virtual reality and Tadao Ando; none of these interventions would have been possible without the idea of my journey, a form that lassoed all these disparate elements together into one structure.

In fact, the essay is a useful format for you to consider; it fits quite successfully with this book's notion of the fragment, the piece. These elements, strung loosely in long, elegant lines (like strings of light bulbs on a cord), cluster well in the essay.

In one group that I ran, I asked the participants to bring an object that they had found on the street. The next week, they described their experiences on these singular journeys; one woman found herself by the river picking up fragments of a burst balloon — all precious elements in her jewel box of emotions.

Zoned down, filtered into now, she was able to experience a clarity of seeing that she had previously not witnessed.

Search out the building site, the abandoned streets, the high-rise view.

Even in your home city, imagine that you are a foreigner.

SMALL, FUTURE

What I am suggesting to you in this third part of the book are techniques that build on the idea of notepad and process.

This might be an approach that is quite the opposite from what you are used to – think of an idea, develop it, make an object, output it (product rather than process).

In my version of creativity, you create a physical field, a net, an internal receiver (via your notepad) that picks up and collects process. These actions don't necessarily offer completed ideas, but instead create a rich landscape out of which, eventually, more original concepts form. It helps you step beyond cliché into a richer terrain.

For example, rather than thinking that you will 'write a novel', you decide to start now, today, with a smaller set of ambitions, 10 minutes each day. Out of this process, that I call 'write myself', a novel might eventually emerge.

It will certainly be a more enjoyable experience – the focus will be on growing and developing your writing skills.

This is 'the big idea myth'; that to start you must have a clear-cut and developed concept, that you advance in strategic stages, step by step, to a completed and commercial goal.

My philosophy is different: small and Eastern – process multiplied by recording equals complexity.

How might you integrate this approach?

One way to avoid 'the big idea myth' is to work physically. In these situations, I'm always influenced by Gestalt.

Gestalt was invented by Fritz and Laura Perls and prioritises an experiential position. Ideas are physically acted out, in the safe space of the therapeutic session, to explore their potential. Since my own background is in these experimental methods, it feels very useful to integrate these procedures.

In my version of creativity, you create a physical field, a net, an internal receiver (via your notepad) that picks up and collects process.

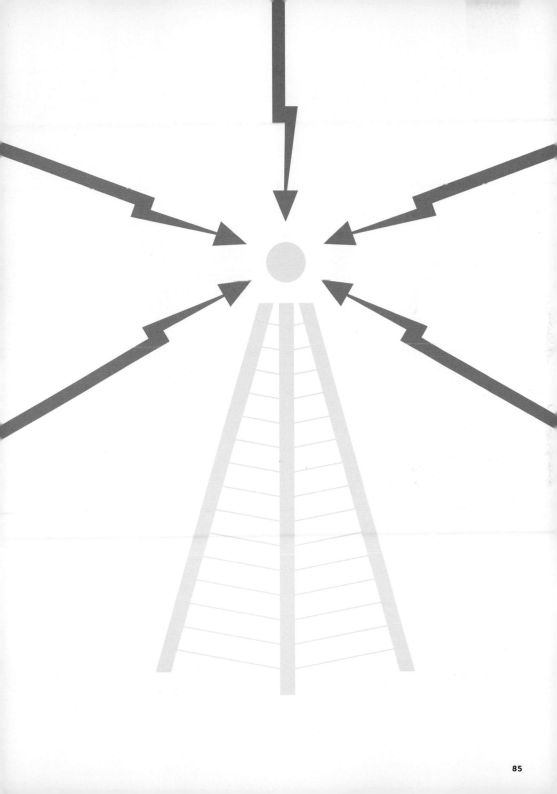

SUPERMARKET RECEIPTS

This physical approach is always exciting; challenging the basic assumptions of creativity. Because when you stand up, when you move, when you walk, you can't stay in the same reality – you have to adapt. Most stuckness comes from stationary positions:

> **Regular office**
> **Usual relationships**
> **Repeated systems**
> **Normal layout**

The beauty of the physical notepad is that it takes you away from the computer screen.

Your current technology is, of course, amazing in what it can achieve. However, it often allows you to present early unformed ideas in a very coherent visual way, with a gloss that is unreal.

The notepad, because it is exceedingly primitive, doesn't offer that – it makes the work more difficult (pieces in contrast, flow ended, radical accidents), but the results can be more exciting and off the wall.

Physicality makes this possible. After all, you are not merely a computer yourself, you are a body moving in space.

Even when I am making work for the computer environment, I tend to make my first 'inside journeys' in my notepad. The tension between the real and the imagined, between the physical notepad and the computer screen, forms a tension that enriches the work.

For example, Google's work on the design language *Material Design* (2014) was made on maquettes of paper and card. Even though the outputs were intended as virtual, they encouraged deep process in their developers by making the models out of physical materials.

One way of achieving this is to integrate a variety of media to express your idea. Use:

Images

Sound recording

Research materials

Notepad pages

Video

(Much of my own writing has been done instantly on supermarket till receipts.)

+ THE EXERCISE

As you assemble your concept from these diverse materials, lay it out on the floor, in flat panels, playing with the relationship between the several items.

Feel free to move things around, inverting the idea, turning it inside out.

Then stand up:

> **What do you see when you look back?**
> **What are the connections, physical and emotional?**
> **What is the perspective that looking down onto the concept gives you?**
> **What do you need to change?**

In this way, you occupy a small future.

Not the grandiosity of distant ideas but the here and now reality of what you have in front of you.

TOOLKIT

09

Persistence is 10 minutes each day – chains of small events, linked together in modular fashion. These long strings of action, evoked over 30 days, provide an essential basis for your creativity.

Driven by your notepad, actioned by observation, these 10 narrowed minutes are the building blocks of your process.

Free up your creative self so that you are open to serendipitous events as they occur all around you.

Don't overthink creativity, just do.

10

Repetition, the regular repeat of action, is now a familiar trope. However, once it was the sole province of the avant-garde. Fifty years later it has been absorbed into the mainstream – however, you can still use its original iteration, as an artist's tool, to develop your creativity.

George Brecht, Linda Montano, Dieter Roth – from Fluxus to performance art. Evoke these methods from the art world to broaden the resources of your practice.

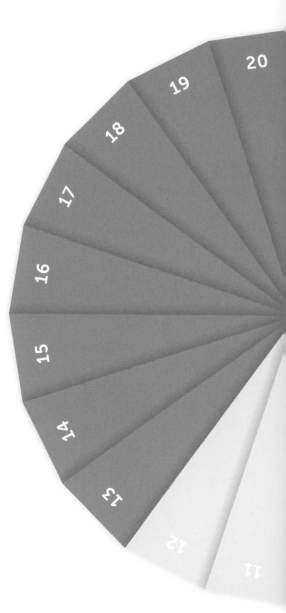

11

Be kind to yourself. The qualities of exploration, curiosity, introspection and enquiry force you away from the harsh world of delivery into a softer space – where you can support yourself and show some self-compassion.

Creativity is not the relentless shovelling of ideas into the void; it can be floating, experimental.

Being 'lost' is one good way of exploring this quality.

12

Creative ideas emerge from process; this regular relationship with your own reality, your own self, is the true source.

Therefore pay attention to process.

Sometimes process leads nowhere; that's OK. Eventually it will build a vast resource that you can draw on every day.

Be patient.

FURTHER LEARNING

READ

Water Yam
George Brecht (Fluxus Editions New York, 1963)

Ando – 1941: The Geometry of Human Space
Masao Furuyama (Taschen 2006)

Out of Now: The Lifeworks of Tehching Hsieh
Adrian Heathfield and Tehching Hsieh (Live Art Development Agency and The MIT Press, 2009)

Dieter Roth: Processing the World
Dieter Roth (Les Presses du Réel, 2014)

Artwords: Discourse on the 60s and 70s
Jeanne Siegel (UMI Research Press, 1985)

CREATE

Card Sets
Build your own set of performance instructions as a homage to artist George Brecht. I use the Silvine brand of lined index cards, which you can find in any stationery shop, but if necessary cut your own out of sheets of white paper. Mark on each one a daily action that you might perform. Then shuffle the pack.

STUDY

QMUL, London, UK
At the School of English and Drama, Queen Mary University of London, the focus is on performance making and active engagement in contemporary practice.

Sacatar Foundation, Itaparica, Brazil
Instituto Sacatar run an international programme of artists' residency fellowships on the island of Itaparica, off the coast of Salvador, Bahia, in Brazil.

VISIT

Confucius Temple
Perform your own Shinto ceremony at Taipei's Confucius Temple in Taipei City, Taiwan. Improvise. I won't give you any further instructions so that I don't inhibit you. The gatekeeper said to me, 'You a movie star?'

Dia Art Foundation
This New York gallery has a programme of contemporary arts.

BEING
RESOURCEFUL

LESSONS

Often we overlook what we have in the rush for the big idea; it's easy to ignore what's right in front of us while we look elsewhere.

Here is the fourth part of the book – in it I will give you further methodologies, tips and techniques to integrate into your practice.

A direct question: how can you develop yourself further?

Often we overlook what we have in the rush for the big idea; it's easy to ignore what's right in front of us while we look elsewhere.

Perhaps there's a useful concept that might be a good place to begin – it could be home, relations, environment, interaction – the simple things that are in front of you.

Creativity is not somewhere else. It is not separate from you; it is you.

Again, I return to the idea of conscious awareness. If you want to be creative, don't be a passenger, a person merely passing through, with a restricted approach to understanding. Challenge yourself to really see beyond the clichés presented to you and use reality, as it actually is, to interrogate these positions.

Often we believe that creativity belongs to other people – these others are the ones who have the right to be creative. I don't support that view. I believe that you are creative. If you continue to place the right to be creative only onto other people, you do yourself a disservice, and diminish your potential.

Creativity is an exploration of what is inside you.

So we will look at the body, at first ideas, as a way of jump-starting your creative life.

Wake up.

PREPARED PIANO

Preparedness is an essential part of your creative toolbox.

Being prepared allows you to be ready, focused, on the page when creativity does arrive. Otherwise these ideas just float by. Similarly, setting up a prepared space, one of opportunity, is an essential methodology. In essence, being prepared is equal to being creative.

As I walk through the city, I keep my 'internal camera' switched on. I see a building being torn down, a cloud of dust, an old brown kitchen flat-packed against the wall, scratches on the bus shelter glass – I store all of these in my prepared space, the open zone of my notepad.

I was introduced to process in my teenage years in an unusual way through the writings of John Cage, particularly his book of lectures and notes *Silence*. I came to his work via experimental music, but the philosophy (Zen Buddhism, chance procedures, Eastern influence) is what stays with me.

I'd like to draw your attention to his work for the prepared piano. It's a good example of process used in a simple way, to create a complex outcome. The prepared piano is an instrument where devices, screws and blocks are placed internally between the strings to give the piano a percussive timbre, quite different in tone from its normal manifestation.

This trick of invention was used to give Cage effects outside the usual Western orchestral range. Yet, ultimately it's still a piano – it can be assembled and put back together.

His skill is in taking what is normal and, using a small, significant twist, moving it towards the exotic.

I still have my vinyl copy of John Cage's 'Sonatas and Interludes for Prepared Piano' (John Tilbury version). As I watch the disc spinning around on the turntable, I remember what it means:

> Adapt reality
> Small steps
> Invent freely
> Upside down
> Make accidents

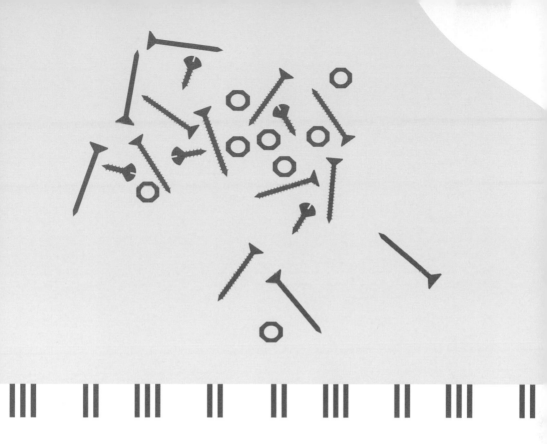

+ THE EXERCISE

Let's see if you can take Cage's approach and apply it to your notepad. For example:

> **Pull it apart**
> **Jump from one written section to another**
> **Tear out several pages**
> **Read from the back**
> **Carry one piece with you each day**

Anything but use it as it is.

Try this very simple alteration: turn your notepad on its side, lengthways, landscape, extending the content of each line across the page. Note how this adapts your working process; by flipping the everyday into the opposite.

Just like Cage, in fact; the conceptual applied to very limited means – not looking for a solution that might revolutionise, but small, sideways moves that alter perception in significant ways.

Avoid the enormity of giant philosophical decisions, but instead make small changes every day.

In this sense, 'prepared' is also a useful state of mind to help you with your creativity.

It suggests that with preparedness you can be ready to grab creativity when it arrives.

The prepared creative senses the opportunity, is open to process, takes small chances, looks inside.

NOTHING HAPPENING

John Cage's lack of efficiency with melody, a quality that hitherto might have excluded him from the Western canon, forced him to turn towards the percussive as the place where he made his work, using instead gamelan dynamics – moving from West to East.

This kind of philosophical shift is very effective, and one that you might adopt.

If you can't work in a conventional format, then think of mood, volume, place, brevity as being your adopted métier. Make a shift from where you have little ability to a new territory, unrelated, to where you can grow.

Rather than meet the block head on, turn sideways to an area of practice where others don't inhabit, giving yourself a better chance of success.

Everyone wants to begin at 'the start', so commence your new idea right at the end, when everyone else has given up.

+ THE EXERCISE

The world of 'the narrative' is always overcrowded; abandon conventional areas of dynamics and try instead:

> **Nothing happening**
> **Empty house**
> **No climax**
> **Everyday activity**
> **Wasted hours waiting**

Rather than meet the block head on, turn sideways to an area of practice where others don't inhabit, giving yourself a better chance of success.

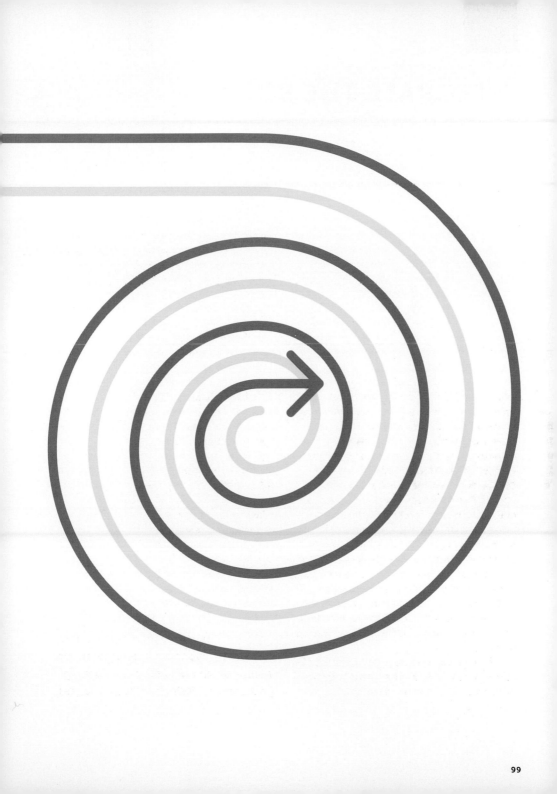

INTEGRATE THE BODY

The body is also a methodology.

Often you can't see it because it's so close to you, but it provides a way of adding process to your creativity, an instant complexity that you can draw on in times of need.

It's the conduit that ties you to yourself.

I've always been influenced by artist Linda Montano's piece with Tehching Hsieh, *Art/Life: One Year Performance 1983–1984*, where Montano and Hsieh spent a year tied to each other by an 8ft rope. This rope suggests to me (among other things) the reality that grounds us in the present moment: the now that we are talking about in this book.

The dedication, commitment, trust and solidity that Montano and Hsieh needed to make this work also recalls, in a much-reduced form, the day-to-day persistence that we all need in order to develop our creativity.

I often think about this rope piece tying us to 'what is'.

For example, when I am making coffee, I am doing nothing but preparing coffee, and when I see cherries in a blue bowl, I am doing nothing but looking at cherries.

The cherries tie me to now, just as the rope tied Montano and Hsieh together.

This idea is helpful in the pursuit of creativity, because it helps you focus on what is directly in front of you, which is usually the most useful concept in the furthering of your idea. So, as my current idea is cherries, I might describe those specific cherries in that exact bowl and write down my detailed description to further stick it to the page.

In the bowl, they look like squirming microbes, so I might take that into my writing, as an extension of my concept.

Whatever is there is the idea.

As I write this book, when I get stuck, I integrate what is in front of me in a direct and unchallenged way — even if it doesn't at first make sense. So, as Linda Montano arrives, I drop her into my text.

Also, prepared piano and microbes, cherries and coffee grains. This improvised way is the only technique that I know that really works. It places you, the creative person, right at the very edge of your potential, working in a live extemporised way with what you have in your internal library.

In a way, it's a method to create a kind of live dreaming, an on-the-edge reverie that brings out the best of you.

However, you don't need to tie a rope around you for 365 days to approximate the ambition and commitment of Linda Montano and Tehching Hsieh. I have found the simple act of standing up also attracts similar energy.

✚ THE EXERCISE

This is an experiment that can easily be applied to a group scenario.

Push the chairs back and ask your participants to stand up. Direct them to find a place in the room that suits their demeanour and mood.

What are they feeling? Invite some responses — why have they chosen to stand in that part of the room? Perhaps it's crowded, or empty. Encourage them to define the contours of the space, and their own choices. Why are they there?

Can they now pin the progress of their creative project onto this positioning?

Often I find that in the most ordinary of conference-room environments, the act of standing up and moving around the space is a truly radical act of subversion, propelling the participants into a fluid space of creative self that knows no limits.

Be careful. Moving from a fixed position physically is an entry point into a more complex setting emotionally, taking on board differences in hierarchy and status. Be prepared for the changes that this philosophical flip can bring.

Always give a limit and time constraint to the experiment. Make sure that you, as the facilitator, also lead by example.

AGE OF IMMATERIALITY

In an age of immateriality, when all around is virtual, accessed via the smart surface of the mobile screen, it's useful to be reminded of our own physical place in the world of substance – what is around us.

Box, page, container, stepladder, amplifier, frame, wood – all objects that I can see in my room.

Like the rope of Montano and Hsieh, these elements tie us to a world of hard surfaces, of persistence. Perhaps what we have been talking about so far in the book has been an attempt to avoid the fantasy of creativity; we are anchoring ourselves in the real, as a way of stepping into the creative.

In the modern world, the idea of 'staying with it' might appear challenging. After all, aren't we always being offered the opportunity of distraction, via shopping, TV, travel, social media? However, you always have one tool that you can use to 'stay': your own body. Only by being in the body can you effect your own change.

+ THE EXERCISE

What does your body feel about your current challenge? Where does it feel it?

Try to locate its centre in the body itself. Is it the:

> **Heart**

> **Arm**

> **Skin**

> **Nerves**

> **Lungs**

> **Foot**

> **Eye**

(Note to self: it can continue to change position as you look.)

Zoom in on this part of the body, as if you were peeling back layers.

You are momentarily at the centre of the block; use this as good information to help you process your current problem. If the heart is central, for example, try to stay with it as you pass through your normal day. Touch your chest from time to time on this important spot to remain connected.

The body anchors you in the present; when you record with your 'internal camera', when you evoke 'process', use the physical as the way into this world.

Breathe in creativity; expel what you don't need, like second-hand smoke.

OFTEN WE
WHAT WE H
THE RUSH
BIG IDEA.

OVERLOOK

AVE IN

FOR THE

FIRST THOUGHTS

Often your first thought is the single most inspired moment. You need go no further than this idea; pull it out, expand, focus on it, elaborate.

Don't go immediately onto the next episode, but stay with what you have.

When I work on my own projects, I insist on these 'stops' – putting in place points where I do not advance. I understand that if I move somewhere else, I am cultivating an avoidance strategy. So I 'stop' and explore the word in all its possibilities (the hard surface of where it is).

Earlier in the book, I gave the example of my 'ESPELIDES' project, an idea that came to me in a dream. Afterwards I could have renamed the website as something else, a more appropriate title, but I left it at a 'stop'. It was only later that I realised

that the first three letters of the name were 'ESP' – something quite appropriate to the clairvoyant nature of the material.

So 'staying with it' can provide further clues if you are willing to dig deep. Ideas grow over time; they are not instant (contrary to opinion), but develop according to process. After several redactions and expansions, crossings-out and word associations, they finally emerge as an original output.

I find that my first thought and my last exhausted exit provide the best ideas.

If you are making recordings, the first grab (when you don't know what you are doing) is often the best, your lack of understanding creating an off-the-wall first take. Or the last attempt (when you are knowledgeable but overwhelmingly tired) is also usually excellent, allowing you the space to let go.

+ THE EXERCISE

Take a title and break it down into component parts. For example, as well as 'ESP', 'ESPELIDES' contains the words 'lid' 'sees', 'lies', 'speed', 'peel', 'deli', 'spies'. What does this tell me about my project?

Do I spy on myself? Is it revelatory? Or can it be about seeing? Visionary potential? Perhaps it's concerned with working fast? Not overthinking an idea? Or, finally, peeling back layers? Showing an essential core? It can be all these things.

Explore all the subsets of your title – as a way of understanding the interior life of your idea, its inner self. Even if these 'workings' never see the light of day, even if they only remain in your notepad, you still stay tuned in, awake, open to the playful elements inside your title. These invisible layers always add a pleasing complexity to any project, a philosophical density that offers depth.

ROOFTOP TO CLOUDS

If you are feeling stuck, blocked from creativity, always head out onto the pavement for inspiration. In a state of exhausted curiosity, everything becomes clear, visible.

Likewise 'guide' versions of any projects, demos or sketches, often provide some core quality that can be absent in later versions. I always go back to my initial napkin scribbles of concepts, keeping them folded between the pages of my notepad. They are like pressed flowers, concentrated energy of the first spark, recorded on paper.

At the end of a project, I return to these maquettes, to see if anything is missing. It's common to lose the forward impetus of an idea in its final manifestation.

A changed word, a corrected title, grammar altered – quickly the character of your work is lost. Be careful of tidying up your drafts too much and integrating conventional syntax.

Character is error.

Allen Ginsberg was the first to coin the phrase 'First thought, best thought'. In doing so, he was referring to his own writing practice and the techniques of his friends Jack Kerouac and William Burroughs; in the Beat Movement, the spontaneous nature of writing was highly valued.

Yet Ginsberg, in this phrase, I believe, was also drawing on a deep seam of Buddhist philosophy. It reminds me of the Rinzai Zen practice of kōans, cryptic questions or dialogues between pupil and master on the subject of non-duality that sometimes offer allusive or obscure answers.

Often these conversations are light and spontaneous. So what A.G.'s phrase 'First thought, best thought' throws up is a quality of improvisation that delivers for the creative an enviable subtlety of touch.

Imagine a book called 'First Thoughts'; what might such a simple volume contain?

First thought is the top of the bus that you are travelling on, or the view from your window; it's where your glance lands – from rooftop, to clouds, to steeple.

In this momentary intuition, every answer can be discerned, or provides a point of entry to further process; the steeple elevates the idea and charges it up like a rocket.

The ideas previously noted in this book:

> **Process**
> **Assisted seeing**
> **Doubles**
> **First thoughts**

are all in a chain, a loop of fission that you follow round and round in your notepad, long lines of DNA. Not one idea, not the ultimate, but instead multiple polymer connections, flickering like light bulbs.

IT'S YOU, HERE

It's easy to think of creativity as 'out there'.

Or the province of others – happening somewhere else in the world – LA, Berlin, London, Taipei.

This 'out there' is simply a projection – it's a way of pushing what you can't hold, out onto others. These 'creatives' are fantasy figures, ideas of the popular imagination that don't really exist. Perhaps this amnesia on your part is in order to elevate these creative individuals beyond you, out of your reach and so keep you passive, locked into a negative relationship with those who can creatively lead.

Of course, there are people who have a lot of creativity, who have developed a skill in this area, who are adept, but it's possible to grow creativity, for you to develop your own creative expertise.

The image I use is practising scales on the piano; it is difficult, but a child can learn it. It's also scalable – it can begin in C, the simplest, and move forward to include more black notes.

Creative skill is possible to develop, step by step.

This book is a guide to that process.

Thinking of creativity as not 'out there' but 'in here', in you, also has another useful advantage, it stops the process of fantasy.

Yes, creativity can be difficult, but you can deal with that difficulty inside you.

You might not become a great artist (who knows what you can do?) but you will, for certain, have a connection with the artist inside you.

Yes, creativity can be difficult, but you can deal with that difficulty inside you. You might not become a great artist (who knows what you can do?) but you will, for certain, have a connection with the artist inside you.

'In C' is also the name of the piece by American composer Terry Riley. The work consists of a score and a set of instructions – 53 small fragments for any number of musicians.

Riley's original approach influenced my own idea of creativity – very simple moves, every day, exercises in writing, clustered together in complex formations; a modular experience. These small parts can be enjoyed for themselves, just writing, or can eventually, over many years, become something that you might want to share with others in the public realm.

However, it is grounded in C, i.e. in the scale of C, in the bedrock of the simplest scale. The 'C' is you, the resources inside of you, the process, the potential for complexity, the step forward.

Summer
Heaven

BAD INFLUENCE

Once, when I was working at a residency in Shanghai, I decided that I would make one simple move every day; I would randomly choose a selection from the *I-Ching* (the Chinese book of divination) and that would be my step. I would record the daily journey that this process allowed. Sometimes these observations were prosaic: crab-flavoured crisps, Robbie Williams' *Greatest Hits*, glass spikes on a wall, while at other times they became philosophical: a crushed alchemy machine, urban metaphysical orientating (UMO).

The trick was that the *I-Ching* often gave me something I didn't want, was bemused by, but because I was locked into my agreed process, my 'C', I had to make something out of these bad choices.

The difficulty provoked movement forwards.

It's a simple reminder; you are the resource for creativity, in all its uncompromising reality.

You might think that you have been given poor chances – the worst office, unsophisticated recording equipment, bad neighbours – yet this is the content of your reality. Think of these elements as pieces of a modular system that you activate each day; over time these become creativity.

The more you theorise about creativity, the more it eludes you.

Valley

Spring
Fire

Thunder

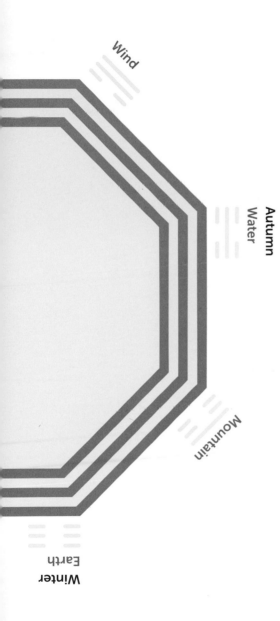

Wind

Autumn
Water

Mountain

Winter
Earth

✛ THE EXERCISE

Make a list now of exactly what you see; all the edges of your negative reality.

Attempt this for the next 30 days. Dig deep into the dirt, the underside, the creases.

Map out the territory of your impoverishment and see what you obtain.

Make a plan of what's currently missing. Mark some A4 pages with simple words on them: 'NO OPTIMISM', 'DIFFICULTY', 'RUBBISH', 'BAD INFLUENCE' and collate them on the floor. When you look back at these startling words, what do you see?

What might allay these worries?

Are there any creative opportunities, or connections that support changes of thinking around your negative feelings?

Build spidery connections between these words, turning 'RUBBISH' into 'RECYCLING'.

If you feel embarrassment when doing some of these exercises, don't push the feeling away, but stay with it: this discomfort of being visible.

I assure you that it will never leave – exposure is central to being creative.

So play with it, become a friend of your exposure, turn towards it slowly, enabling a dialogue with the visibility.

You are 'it'.

TOOLKIT

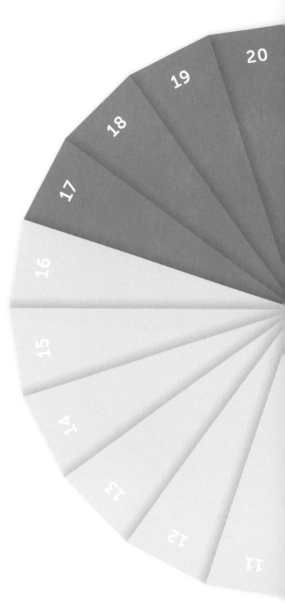

13

'Prepared' is a useful state of mind, placing you like a net to receive ideas, as you might capture data or radio signals. This action involves simple means, it is not sophisticated and can be easily achieved – for example, turning your notepad on its side, or reducing the size of a page.

John Cage's prepared piano is a good example of this technique: using minor alterations to a classic (the pianoforte) to achieve percussive results.

14

The body is a useful resource, moving you beyond your ego to a more considered place, grounded and pragmatic. Use your own body as part of your toolkit, to help you make decisions – remember, it's also a portable device.

Instead of immediately looking for answers from technology, use the idea of 'staying with it', making a choice to listen to your own body, your own intuition.

The body is itself a technology.

15

First (or last) thoughts often hold something magic about them; without understanding with certainty what exactly you are doing, you can sometimes step beyond logic, into a creative space.

Go back to your original notes – the improvisations, the words on the page – to see if anything has been lost in moving from the original idea to final product.

What is missing?

Try and unlearn the rules that you took so long to master.

16

Don't believe that creativity is 'out there', beyond yourself; it is inside you.

Exposure is central to being creative – that won't change with experience. You will always be in the middle of mess, with embarrassment, difficult feelings. Instead of fighting this experience, use it as a tool. Remind yourself each day that you have some responsibility for your creativity.

You can change things.

FURTHER LEARNING

READ

Silence: Lectures and Writings
John Cage (Marion Boyars, 1973)

Jack Kerouac and Allen Ginsberg:
The Letters Jack Kerouac and Allen Ginsberg,
edited by Bill Morgan and David Stanford
(Viking Penguin, 2010)

Letters from Linda M. Montano
Linda M. Montano, edited by Jennie Klein
(Routledge 2005)

Experimental Music: Cage and Beyond
Michael Nyman (Studio Vista, Cassell and
Collier Macmillan, 1974)

I-Ching or Book of Changes
Translated by Richard Wilhelm and Cary
F. Baynes, with a foreword by C.G. Jung
(Routledge & Kegan Paul, 1951)

EXPLORE

The Wire
Subscribe to *The Wire* magazine, a monthly
vehicle for underground and experimental
music. Alternatively listen to its weekly radio
show on London's Resonance FM.

STUDY

Tate Modern Tanks, London, UK
The underground tanks were the original
oil storage facility when Tate was a working
power station. Visit the space to focus
your attention on performance and works
outputted live. The Tate Public Programmes
also run many courses, linked to visiting
exhibitions. Sign up to one of the workshops.

VISIT

Paterson
Take a trip to Paterson, New Jersey, USA, the
place where Allen Ginsberg spent his youth.
While there, imagine what kind of work you
might have to make nowadays to create the
equivalent to that of the Beat Writers. If you
can't afford the trip, imaginatively create your
own environment where these situations
become real. Likewise, explore William S.
Burroughs (Tangier, Morocco) and Jack
Kerouac (Lowell, Massachusetts) as similar
sites for creativity.

CHALLENGES & DIFFICULTY

LESSONS

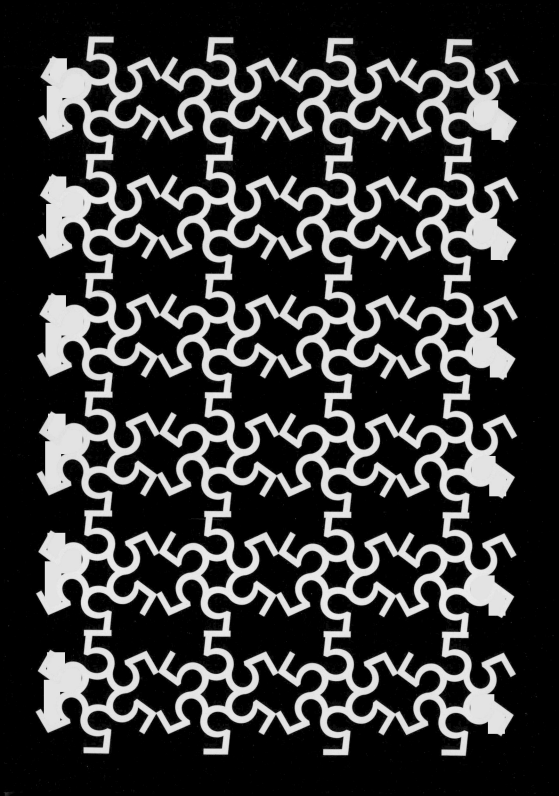

Don't 'feel the fear' — this idea has merely become cliché. Instead, take the opposite approach and make a friend of all anxieties — that's my philosophy.

Here is the last part of the book — it's concerned with endings: the section that is about finishing projects, coming to a close, fixing an end point.

And so, the question remains: how to conclude?

Again, I return to a major theme in the book — what impact it has on you.

Endings, surprisingly, are more complex than beginnings — anyone can start; the blank page is there for the grasping, but fewer creatives can package and design a format that successfully finalises their outputs.

Without endings, you are simply floating, finding no focus, searching endlessly — endings provide borders, stability, rigidity. (Sometimes a little solidity is just what you need.)

Of course, the difficulty with endings is that 'finality' brings up different feelings for each of us — vulnerability, lack of confidence, even frailty. The end point puts pressure on the soft part that responds to personal criticism.

Therefore, endings can unleash personal challenges that push you to the limit.

As in all parts of this book, the solution is to explore in detail what it means, attempting to integrate the fear of endings back into your work — folding doubt and awareness into the product. This approach always adds complexity.

Don't 'feel the fear' — this idea has merely become cliché. Instead, take the opposite approach and make a friend of all anxieties — that's my philosophy.

THE FINISH

It's hard to admit, but often a large portion of your time and energy will be used up in ending a project.

Beginning is optimistic, capricious, wayward, voluminous, a place where everything is possible, while endings are difficult, hard-edged, depressive; the chance to invent becomes limited, you are forced to offer a premature finish.

Edits mean sacrifice.

When I am faced with this challenge, I remind myself that endings are a part of life. We see it in nature all the time – the to and fro of plants and humans. In fact, conclusion gives meaning to our lives.

If you are stuck with endings, try the following exercise which translates the intellectual difficulty of finishing into a visual piece of process.

+ THE EXERCISE

In your mind's eye, imagine that you are positioned at one single point in time.

This might be an image – a feather, a stone, a lever, a seed pod, a rock. Whatever feels appropriate to this moment.

Use the exercise of the 'internal camera' to help you; remember that you are recording what's inside, right now.

Gradually extend this sense of self beyond the instant of difficulty, forward towards a moment of dissolution. See the room fade, the walls expand, the body empty, the days extend. Yet also keep your awareness of your own presence in this wider vision. The fluctuation of time – the insect speck of this current problem.

When you return, write a note from this bigger self, located in the wider universe, to the smaller self that had the original problem.

'Dear diary...'

Why does this exercise work?

It helps because it locates you in a bigger idea of the world, not limited to your specific challenge. Your project can be chopped, adapted, revised, chainsawed (just like a tree for wood) because all things are open to change:

> **Your page can be folded**
> **Scissors are at hand**
> **The water glass can be up-ended**
> **Pages can be scrapped**

Because endings are so huge, with echoes for us of the infinite, of finality, they are difficult to penetrate. This exercise reminds you that it's OK to interrogate these 'deaths'.

Creativity is, in fact, constant change.

On my desk I have a rhombus-shaped piece of black obsidian — a type of igneous rock.

When I'm faced with an ending, I hold it and feel the older time structure of its making seep into my hand and body.

This is a conscious echo of an idea from NLP (neuro-linguistic programming) — the notion of 'anchors'. In this technique, an object or a touch can trigger a prefigured emotion that might help you in a moment of challenge. For example, placing an index finger in the palm of your opposite hand could trigger a feeling of solidity.

This is a particularly useful method for counteracting the instability that endings provide. Rocks are often helpful in providing this grounded feeling because they have a robust, enduring quality. They hold the ground.

PRIMITIVE TOOL

In one recent workshop, I was looking for an object to use as a check-in with the group but I couldn't find something appropriate among my belongings. However, on a walk to the supermarket, following a curving path by the lake that took in a shopping centre and the local cemetery, I came across a stone that I thought might have the requisite qualities:

> **Hard**
> **Primitive tool**
> **Weighted**
> **Volcanic energy**

It had many of the 'edges' we were trying to encourage in our work together.

By accident, it also had the flavour of endings, via the church's graveyard, positioned at the edge of town, just like the other shopping experience across the dual carriageway, but this time of a different nature and timescale – the final rebuttal.

The rock allowed me to tolerate this bigger vista: to wait, to look more completely, to see what might happen, to feel embodied.

These 'energetic' solutions of NLP and stones might appear impractical for the dynamic, modern world of business and enterprise.

However, stay with the idea. You are often stuck because you are following very familiar routes of creative endeavour, the set way of doing things. Integrating instinct in this way forces you to reassess your contribution.

You are otherwise just recycling cliché.

If this feels like the case, try to support your own instinctive responses by offering a blanket ban on media for 24 hours; longer, if you can keep it up. Don't open any news site or switch on the TV. In this empty space, gladly given, what can you really see?

In this new area of self-discovery, what constitutes an appropriate ending?

> **A visual map?**
> **A hundred opinions?**
> **A single word?**
> **An image?**

Reports or final documentation often slavishly follow one set route. With your new ideas of ending, what can you discover that might make the outputs less stereotypical?

+ THE EXERCISE

Find an object that adds solidity to your ending.	Do you need weight, purpose, definition? Or softness, vulnerability, change?

Try to support your own instinctive responses
by offering a blanket ban on media for 24 hours; longer,
if you can keep it up.

Off

Off

DIY

I've left the most important piece of advice for the last part of the book.

Do it yourself.

In these three simple words, I encapsulate all of my creative career. I'll elaborate: don't wait for anyone else to offer approval. Do it now without delay. Make it happen.

Do I need to say more?

Do it now.

DIY is a powerful vehicle to push you forward into your potential. Your progress might be difficult, but you will be carried by the force of your own self – and you will never face the opprobrium of someone else.

In the previous lessons, I've encouraged you to explore your own process. It's possible for you to take on board all of this guidance, but in the confusion created by endings, throw all this awareness away – too eager to finish, too willing to extinguish the difficulty.

In this moment, you might consider giving all your power to another.

It's an undeniable feature of individual creativity that in the last stretch we often give up and can't complete the work. The project sometimes feels too overwhelming, too complex.

We say:

> **Please give me money**
> **Output my work**
> **Take control of my finances**
> **Be my manager**

Please don't surrender to these impulses; do it yourself.

These are abnegations of self; sleights of hand that seem to improve things, but often don't achieve a lot. It's your own voice, hands, sight, thoughts, steps that can make a difference.

I will say it once again for emphasis: do it yourself. There is no other attitude that is more magnetic than:

> **I can do it**
> **I can take a risk**
> **I have the personal resources**
> **I can make it work**

These are powerful, self-identifying behaviours, which through their enthusiasm, attract other people.

When I have stepped out and made projects based solely on my own joy, without recourse to backers, these ventures have always proved the most successful, fuelled by my own energy and candour.

DIY is a powerful
vehicle to push
you forward into
your potential.
Your progress
might be
difficult, but you
will be carried by
the force of your
own self.

EMPTY WALL

The output is important; it will move your practice forward. Even if the release is small, numbering tens of copies, still publicly announce the versions.

If you are an artist, publish your work in small editions of photocopied pamphlets, four pages or less, and distribute these for free in coffee shops and urban arcades. Sell them outside concerts; or barter, negotiate.

This is exactly how I started my publishing trajectory – not with editions of thousands but with low-cost, portable editions that I could carry with me at all times. I was inspired by the example of artist Keith Haring, who began his career on the New York subway, drawing in chalk on the empty black panels, the vacant wall spaces awaiting advertisements. (Haring was often fined for vandalism.) I recall years later, wandering into a gallery in Paris, quite by accident, and seeing his Mickey Mouse drawings: images that have stayed with me, on the fringes of my memory for a long time.

This enterprising attitude has always motivated me to notice where other people are not looking – found spaces, on the edge of what is seen; the illegitimate becomes the legitimate once someone stakes a claim on it. So get in quick and make your mark.

+ THE EXERCISE

Look for spaces that might support an intervention.

Don't search out the grandest, most visible canvas, but instead a place that is instantly achievable and available:

> **Wastepaper bin**
> **Your front window**
> **Empty wall**
> **Your own hand**

I'm always inspired by Cildo Meireles' *Insertions into Ideological Circuits: Coca-Cola Project* (1970), common fizzy pop bottles re-inscribed with incendiary statements and introduced back into circulation. This appears to me to be a genuine, funny, explosive way of dealing with the idea of mass production. The idea of taking on a corporate power and overturning it is both facetious and exciting.

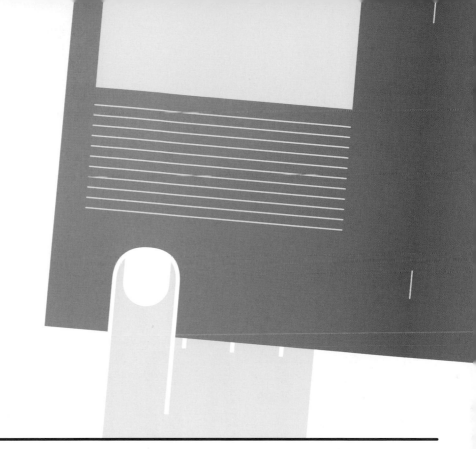

The lesson of DIY is that you don't always need to wait for permission. In some projects, no one will give it to you. Instead, make an entry in unexpected and oblique ways.

Refuse to get sucked into existing norms of production – 'good' quality is often a way of controlling. If necessary, photocopy it, or record it on low-res video (whatever's to hand).

Just get it out now.

These strategies position you as an outsider, willing to take a chance on your own creativity, unapologetic about being visible.

But be careful. If you decide to do it all yourself, there will be no manager, gallery or publisher to protect you. A game of hide-and-seek, using these elements, is often the best approach to protect yourself:

> Full visibility
> Anonymity
> Step forward
> Group identity
> Disguise

As you plunge into DIY, it's a good idea to save 10% of the project for you, a small shadow to retreat to if things become difficult.

That 10% could save your life.

CREATIVITY
IN FACT, CO
CHANGE.

IS,
NSTANT

END WITH CONFUSION

One way of moving on is to make endings themselves into a creative act.

Accept that it will be messy and be prepared to adapt, right up to the last minute. In this way, you are not cornered by endings, but stand resolute, ready to change.

Try it this way:

+ THE EXERCISE

Take any document that you are currently working on and print it out in a variety of coloured papers. Don't think too much about which page should be with what colour. Trust that the results will work.

Next, sequence the printed-out pages so that all the 'yellows' or 'greens', instead of being consecutive as they came out of the printer, numbered as normal, are all clustered together.

Don't worry if this doesn't make sense.

Finally, look at the group of colours. As you jump from one 'yellow' page to another, as you read sentences that weren't meant to be side by side, do you notice anything?

Does anything make sense, by not making sense? Does it offer you a new reading?

This exercise works by taking away some of the inevitability of endings, and making it into a game. With this colour technique you pin elements next to each other that have no previous formal relationship, so you keep fluid, refusing to stay solid.

Things can still change; you can make an agreement with yourself that it's still possible.

This drop into confusion, especially at the end of a project, subverts the neat endings that you might anticipate and meets the finish head on.

I find this really helps – interrogating the chaos of the end with your own chosen confusion.

I've stopped looking for clever answers in endings; I find the last stretch of a project, the final 2%, to be destabilising, odd, unsympathetic, messy. I now accept that it will not be otherwise, and don't live in the fantasy of revelatory finishes.

In fact, if there's one central message of this book, it is this: abandon the illusion of creativity. Instead, address what's there. This also applies to endings. Deal with 'what is'; say 'goodbye' to the work and move on.

Be free of the mess.

My own creative trail is littered with abandoned projects, small ideas that didn't grow, or completed works that were never outputted. It's a breaker's yard of old vehicles, items that no longer run and that are taken apart for scrap.

I have various folders on my desktop that I drop these projects into: 'Elastic', 'The Walk Tower', 'Experiment 1', 'Datalog for Cheops' – some quite useful ideas (some of these folders are in fact empty). They are like cast-offs, the results of process that didn't work.

But, of course, they have a function; they fuel creativity by providing a rich soil, a dirt out of which things grow.

Occasionally, I will dip into these digital files and pluck out a word, or an idea, that can be integrated into my current work, a loose vortex of new and old.

Creativity is 'elastic experiment', an evolving zone where the hard boundaries of logic only sometimes apply.

ALADDIN'S CAVE

Your fear of endings might be allayed by these processes – use the experimental approach to allow you to remain lithe, flexible.

This randomising of old and new, a dip into the Aladdin's cave of the unconscious, is a technique that is really useful to wrap up a project. If you can't decide where to end, try allowing forces outside of you to make that choice:

> **Nature**
> **Other people**
> **Chance**
> **Rapid endings**

Thus you meet the horror of ending with your own confusion; make it part of creativity itself.

Recently, on the London Underground I found an abandoned copy of J.D. Salinger's *The Catcher in the Rye* – the edition with the 1970s silver Penguin cover. J.D. haunts this version of 'Being Creative', cropping up a few times during the writing of the book. I took the discovery as a sign that something important was contained within this volume.

What I enjoy about *The Catcher in the Rye* is the sly undermining of the literary classic, like the wry take on page one (by the main character Seymour) on Dickens' writing.

I was finding myself stuck searching for an ending to my own book, so I tried an old

technique and opened the book at random. I landed on page 117, another breezy riff on the dry world of literature – Shakespeare's *Romeo and Juliet* (it wasn't without irony that I remembered *The Catcher in the Rye* is now on most school exam board reading lists alongside the bard's own work).

How might I integrate Seymour's own iconoclastic opinions about *Romeo and Juliet* into the last part of this project?

The first thing to recognise is that the finding of the book had already taken me on an 'internal journey'. Secondly, I was willing to adopt the novel discovery as a tool, integrating my own 'process', my 'internal camera' – I used the book, its shiny silver cover, as a mirror to reflect parts of myself.

(This consciousness of my own process is already a large part of the solution; consciousness multiplied by process equals creativity – as seen already in Part Three of the book.)

If I thought about 'Romeo' and 'Juliet' as being diverse parts of myself in conflict, 'masculine' and 'feminine', archetypal figures, the lead characters that needed to be brought together in a union to complete my work, I could then think about using that rivalry as part of the process of ending.

Of course, *Romeo and Juliet* doesn't end in union but in misinformation and death.

Perhaps living with confusion is necessary to the creative process.

Sometimes it just doesn't work out.

SAY 'GOODBYE'

It's necessary to say 'goodbye' to your creative work in order to give it meaning.

The brutal output that is the book/ performance/record/exhibition forces you to leave your ideas behind and move on. You might not be ready to do that; you might protest, but ultimately it's good for you.

Without endings, you can remain immured in making forever. The closed door, slammed shut, has its place.

Often, we keep the project in motion with several balls juggling to avoid a hard exit. If creativity is the 'self', the finish is the 'death' of your project – an ending that arrives despite the fact that your idea might not be properly realised or accurate.

You must live with 'incomplete', the 'good enough' project.

In most instances, no fairy-tale endings are present; sometimes your work doesn't explore its full potential. You need to continue despite the unfulfilled expectations, the loss, and leave it behind.

Yet, remember my previous assertion that creativity is modular – within this framework, there are 'wins' and 'failures'. The rhizome-like nature of process is that, sooner or later, after a 'loss' another 'success' will arrive.

You have to take these quiet times of 'loss' in your stride and move on.

The waves of creativity (remember them, from Part One?), that can occur in each 24 hours, test your humility by throwing failure at you, just to challenge your deepest capability.

If you can weather the storm, you can call yourself an artist.

In fact, praying to the gods of failure is not a bad thing to do.

We focus on success so much – the shimmering, illusive object of desire – that it's good occasionally to celebrate our defeat, lack of ability, melancholy or bad fortune.

I recall that in some cultures, instead of dealing with the plagues of ants that constantly surround food, the insects are given their own meals, away from the house, to appease them. This seems accurate – the old gods of Shinto, of the forest, of light, celebrate with us and mourn our losses.

If you don't succeed, worry less – there will be another day.

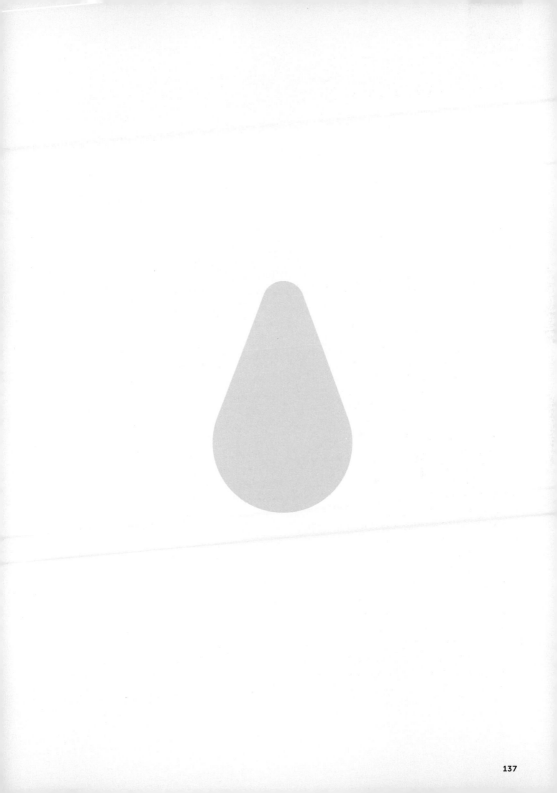

NEW EYES

The main thing is to propel your heart into your work — this is, I admit, easier said than done.

We have seen in the book how we default to the cliché, habit and formulas — routines that stop us from working authentically or accurately. If you take one thing away from the book, try and see yourself with new eyes

This can be done in small ways.

Practise every day by rehearsing personal endings:

> **Lock the door to the office**
> **Switch off the computer**
> **Throw the page in the waste bin**
> **Lose the TV remote**

Do these with the express intention of coming to a close, forcing an ending, expressing a need to come to an unforeseen conclusion.

In this way you might practise finishes. Not the big Hollywood acceptance speech that you might be rehearsing in your head, but the smaller note to self:

> **It worked well**
> **I survived**
> **I learned something**
> **It had a good 'take-away'**
> **I transcended limits**
> **It cohered**

Often in client-facing situations, at the moment of ending I interrogate myself and allow a small check-in.

What did I learn from this situation?

(The answer can be unrelated to the quality or the success of the project.)

What did I learn about myself?

Thus we come back, full-circle, to process, that little word that hangs over much of this book, like a bright-yellow umbrella.

What can you take away?

+ THE EXERCISE

Write down now in your notepad what you can extrapolate from this chapter.

Is there a feeling? Is it one word? What does your 'internal camera' record from the reading of this book?

I might evoke journey metaphors here — struggle, success. I could even talk about mountains and ambition. What are they there for: to understand that there are some things that even we can't conquer.

Not the ambitions of gleaming, endless achievement but modest moving forward.

One step in front of the other. A daily practice of notepad, methodologies, process, dialogue, pen. These might not meet your fantasies of what creativity is, but they are achievable.

You develop a practice that is real, ambitious, complex, sustainable.

I encourage you to stay with yourself as the only source of creativity — it's not out there, but inside you.

You are the receptacle of all things creative.

TOOLKIT

17

Outputs are necessary in order to develop
your own creativity, even if the endings
are awkward, incomplete. You must leave
something behind and move on in order to
step forward, to grow.

These endings have a powerful echo for
us of our own finite qualities – and so evoke
complex feelings. They are not merely the
output of a project, but trigger archetypal
emotions.

It feels like 'everything' is 'over' but it's just
another form of beginning.

18

DIY is a way of taking back control, directing
your own outputs. Here you are answerable
to no one. The power of saying 'I can do
this', 'I can sell this' is inestimable – DIY can
change your life.

Don't wait for permission, just get on with
it yourself.

You can make very small outputs, in
primitive old formats, that can still move
things forward.

19

The finish will be confusing, but meet it head on with your own creative chaos, scissors in hand. Accept that it will be messy, and be prepared to adapt, right up to the last minute.

Often old notepads can provide sources of inspiration to unblock you. Flip through a book, or pull in another influence, quite different from the one that you are working on. Integrate colour information or visual imagery to accelerate change.

20

You must say 'goodbye' to the work in order to move ahead.

Live with the 'incomplete' project, output the idea and leave it behind. This hard exit, this lack of fairy tale, of fantasy, is necessary for creativity. Not every idea will be 100% successful.

Move on.

Explore failure and success equally; these are your twin objectives — each has a useful formula to add to your leaving.

FURTHER LEARNING

READ

***Extreme Metaphors: Selected Interviews
with J.G. Ballard, 1967–2008***
J.G. Ballard, edited by Simon Sellars and Dan
O'Hara (Fourth Estate, 2012)

***Miracles of Life: Shanghai to Shepperton –
An Autobiography***
J.G. Ballard (Fourth Estate, 2008)

Against Nature
Joris-Karl Huysmans (Penguin Classics, 1959)

The Catcher in the Rye
J.D. Salinger (Hamish Hamilton, 1951)

Mrs Dalloway
Virginia Woolf (Hogarth Press, 1925)

Publishing details are based on the first UK edition,
except in cases where there is no similar and
therefore a USA version is appended.

STUDY

Birkbeck, London, UK
Short evening courses at Birkbeck, University
of London, Department of English and
Humanities. The focus is on cultural enquiry
and interdisciplinary debates.

INVEST

Black Food
Integrate the approach of Huysmans'
decadent classic *Against Nature* by staying
with the inverse of what's expected
(Huysmans suggested a banquet of black
food). By aligning your creativity with the
opposite of what's obvious, you might come
up with some surprising results, the essential
flip that gives your product market leverage.

VISIT

Foyles
Spend some time in the Art and Architecture
Department of Foyles Bookshop, London.
Browse, purchase or merely look. Duplicate
this approach with any local gallery
bookshop. The idea is to fill yourself up with
inspiration, to absorb the visual environment.

Magma
This independent shop specialises in design,
small editions and magazines.

EPILOGUE

The introduction to this book focuses on the word 'being' in the title, a natural state of creativity that we all own: this curiosity, the playfulness is our childhood inheritance. We can all access it every day.

It's also true that this book has largely concerned itself with your 'internal camera', process, as a way of accessing creativity. This approach aligns with my position as a Jungian – I'm always hoping to grow your internal life, your awareness.

But as I finish, I also recall that the exterior world is equally important: creativity resides in action. Our innate creative state of being must be activated, regularly utilised in order to develop it.

I'm reminded of J.G. Ballard's assertion that no person in a Virginia Woolf novel ever filled up a car with a tank of petrol. Meaning: don't only think of the inside, look outside to the world. Note down the details of your external life, as you find them.

In the 20th century (post-Freud and the arrival of psychoanalysis), we have largely concentrated on the internal space, but there is a wide world of experience out there to be mapped, recorded. For example, if you could describe a trip to the contemporary supermarket to buy a packet of breakfast cereal, with all its modern hyper-reality, or the insertion of a bank card into a slot in the wall, with its concurrent bodily connotations (step back and see it as it is, for a moment), then you might be truly creative.

In fact, it's the collision of these two – inside reality and outside awareness – where creativity exists.

Reading back through the book, I'm also struck how artists from my own past enter as 'characters' – John Cage, Shunryu Suzuki, J.D. Salinger. Like in a play, they slide in and out, as if in my own toy theatre.

I'm glad that I've taken this approach. Many books on creativity suggest a series of principles, a set of rules that must be followed. In contrast, I've shown how my own

In the 20th century (post-Freud and the arrival of psychoanalysis) we have largely concentrated on the internal space, but there is a wide world of experience out there to be mapped, recorded.

struggles with creativity have unfolded – not from a position of omniscience but using my feet on the ground to guide me practically.

What I'm suggesting with this polymath approach is that whatever my eye or ear lands on 'is' my creativity. This is not mere solipsism – the same is true for you.

What you look at 'is' yourself, and as a consequence your creativity.

Bring your own 'characters' to life. Record anything that draws your attention: this might be your mantra. Collect what you see and hear.

The radical self is your future.

The world of creativity is not a series of abstract, mathematical principles, a data set that can be rigorously applied. It is formed from your enthusiasm, persistence, willingness, uniqueness. If you develop your own self, your creativity will naturally flourish.

It's this path that you must follow at the end of the book.

Good luck.

NOTES

At BUILD+BECOME we believe in building knowledge that helps you navigate your world.

Our books help you make sense of the changing world around you by taking you from concept to real-life application through 20 accessible lessons designed to make you think. Create your library of knowledge.

BUILD + BECOME

www.buildbecome.com
buildbecome@quarto.com

@buildbecome
@QuartoExplores

Using a unique, visual approach, Gerald Lynch explains the most important tech developments of the modern world – examining their impact on society and how, ultimately, we can use technology to achieve our full potential.

From the driverless transport systems hitting our roads to the nanobots and artificial intelligence pushing human capabilities to their limits, in 20 dip-in lessons this book introduces the most exciting and important technological concepts of our age, helping you to better understand the world around you today, tomorrow and in the decades to come.

Gerald Lynch is a technology and science journalist, and is currently Senior Editor of technology website TechRadar. Previously Editor of websites Gizmodo UK and Tech Digest, he has also written for publications such as *Kotaku* and *Lifehacker,* and is a regular technology pundit for the BBC. Gerald was on the judging panel for the James Dyson Award. He lives with his wife in London.

GERALD LYNCH

BUILD + BECOME

GET TECHNOLOGY

BE IN THE KNOW.
UPGRADE YOUR FUTURE.

KNOW TECHNOLOGY TODAY, TO EQUIP YOURSELF FOR TOMORROW.

Using a unique, visual approach to explore philosophical concepts, Adam Ferner shows how philosophy is one of our best tools for responding to the challenges of the modern world.

From philosophical 'people skills' to ethical and moral questions about our lifestyle choices, philosophy teaches us to ask the right questions, even if it doesn't necessarily hold all the answers. With 20 dip-in lessons from history's great philosophers alongside today's most pioneering thinkers, this book will guide you to think deeply and differently.

Adam Ferner has worked in academic philosophy both in France and the UK – but it's philosophy *outside* the academy that he enjoys the most. In addition to his scholarly research, he writes regularly for *The Philosophers' Magazine*, works at the Royal Institute of Philosophy and teaches in schools and youth centres in London.

ADAM FERNER

BUILD + BECOME

THINK DIFFERENTLY

OPEN YOUR MIND.
PHILOSOPHY FOR
MODERN LIFE.

PHILOSOPHY IS ABOUT
OUR LIVES AND HOW WE
LIVE THEM.

CATHERINE BLYTH

BUILD+
BECOME

ENJOY TIME

STOP RUSHING.

BE MORE PRODUCTIVE.

October 2018

NATHALIE SPENCER

BUILD+
BECOME

GOOD MONEY

BE IN THE KNOW.

BOOST YOUR

FINANCIAL WELL-BEING.

October 2018

Using a unique, visual approach to explore the science of behaviour, *Read People* shows how understanding why people act in certain ways will make you more adept at communicating, more persuasive and a better judge of the motivations of others.

The increasing speed of communication in the modern world makes it more important than ever to understand the subtle behaviours behind everyday interactions. In 20 dip-in lessons, Rita Carter translates the signs that reveal a person's true feelings and intentions and exposes how these signals drive relationships, crowds and even society's behaviour. Learn the influencing tools used by leaders and recognise the fundamental patterns of behaviour that shape how we act and how we communicate.

Rita Carter is an award-winning medical and science writer, lecturer and broadcaster who specialises in the human brain: what it does, how it does it, and why. She is the author of *Mind Mapping* and has hosted a series of science lectures for public audience. Rita lives in the UK.

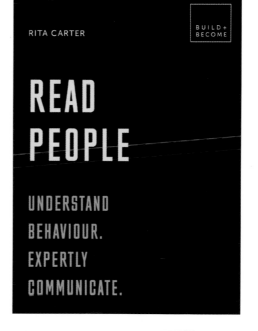

RITA CARTER

BUILD +
BECOME

READ
PEOPLE

UNDERSTAND
BEHAVIOUR.
EXPERTLY
COMMUNICATE.

CAN YOU SPOT A LIE?

01
BUILD +
BECOME

FIRST IMPRESSIONS

You already have the ability to read faces; it's built right into your brain. The skill is so important that we have evolved a brain system dedicated to face-reading and it works with astonishing speed. Before we are even conscious of seeing a person, an ancient, hard-wired cognitive system makes a complex judgement about them based on the shape, form, proportions and expressions of their face. It decides first whether the person is attractive or repellent, and then whether they are competent, trustworthy, extrovert or dominant.

Do you know that feeling of distrust or recoil when you meet a stranger, even one who is behaving impeccably? If you don't, it's probably because you override your seemingly inexplicable intuitions about people, preferring to concentrate on more rational ways of judging them.

Instant reaction (unconscious):
One tenth of a second
Conscious reaction:
0.5–10 seconds

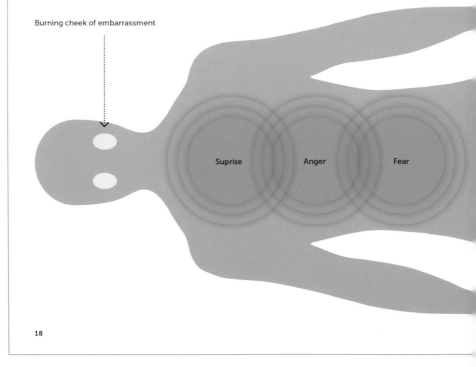

Burning cheek of embarrassment

Suprise   Anger   Fear

18

Gut reactions seem to come from nowhere and be based on nothing. They can't be assessed or double-checked, and they happen as a result of calculations that are not accessible to us – processes we may not even know are happening. It seems irrational to take any notice of them

In fact, there is a very good reason to note them. The ability to make instant, largely unconscious judgements about faces has proved so useful to us that evolution has written it into our genes. It is our primary strategy for distinguishing between friend and foe but, like most of our built-in defences, it is pretty crude. Yet, intuitive face-reading has stuck in our genes because – on the whole – it works.

Confronted with an unfamiliar face, you will make quite a complex judgement about its owner within one tenth of a second. Your brain will judge whether the person is trustworthy, attractive, likeable, competent, aggressive or peaceable. All of this happens before you know consciously that you have seen them! When the face stays in view long enough to make a conscious judgement (from half a second to 10 seconds), your initial judgement is unlikely to change significantly. The only big difference is that you get more confident about it. First impressions are not only fast – they last. We refer to 'gut reactions' because our digestive tract is massively endowed with nervous tissue which reacts intensely to emotional events. Emotions are also felt throughout the body: think of the 'burning cheeks' of embarrassment, the 'weak knees' of foreboding, or the trembling hand of anxiety. Even gut reactions are different according to the emotion experienced: fear is frequently felt quite low in the abdomen, while anger is felt higher up, in the stomach or above.

Trembling hand of anxiety

Weak knees of foreboding

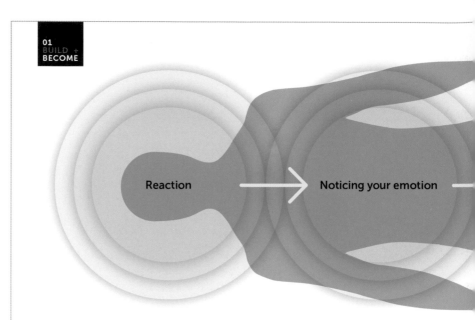

01
BUILD +
BECOME

Reaction → Noticing your emotion →

SNAP JUDGEMENTS

For many of us, making snap judgements feels wrong. Our initial feeling about a person tends to be fleeting and easily drowned out by the subsequent onslaught of information we receive as we interact with them. We may not notice a tiny flutter of fear or attraction or, if we do, we may dismiss it as meaningless. This is a mistake, but it is one that is frequently made by many of us.

Indeed, the judgements we make instantly are very likely to be the same as those made by people who know the person well.

You don't have to know how the face-reading brain trick works to make it work for you. When you meet someone new, you can enhance your natural face-reading skills by attending to your own feelings and behaviour, as well as to those of the other person.

First, get familiar with your emotions. Start by noting when you have an emotion that you experience physically – butterflies

or a spontaneous frown, for instance. Emotional thoughts are just side shoots of emotion, the core of them is an alteration in body state.

Next, identify the emotion and put a name to it. Don't limit yourself to the obvious ones like joy, anger, fear and so on; recognize the hybrids too – the mixture of fear and elation you get before a fairground ride, or the combined sadness and sweetness of nostalgia. Once you have identified what emotion you are feeling, take time to examine exactly what physical effect it is having on you.

Although emotions produce typical physical reactions, we are all slightly different, so learn to identify your own responses. When I am fearful, I feel two small cold patches just below my cheekbones. A friend of mine says she feels fear in her upper arms.

20

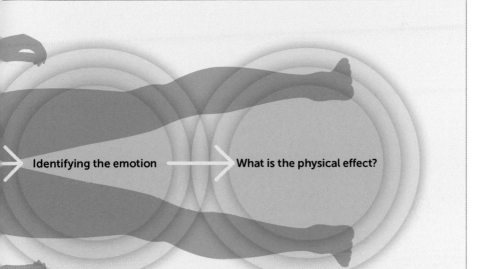

Identifying the emotion ➝ **What is the physical effect?**

Now scrutinize your biases. Some people are very sensitive to threat, while others are exceedingly trusting. And life events – abuse at the hands of a person with a particular type of face, say – can alter one's reactions to such a face, even at an unconscious level.

So, while you should always take note of your reactions, you should also factor in these biases: if you know you habitually feel fear at the sight of a stranger, try overriding your intuition just a little.

In one study researchers asked volunteers to gauge the competence of a lecturer on the basis of a two-second clip of the teacher talking. Their quick-fire verdicts more or less matched the judgements of students who had been taught by the professors for an entire term. The same group have shown that the leadership ability of corporation bosses can be assessed surprisingly accurately by a glance at their photo. They asked volunteers to look at pictures of chief executives of the top

25 and the bottom 25 companies in the Fortune 1,000 list and judge how good they thought the person they were looking at would be at leading a company.

The results of their study showed that the students' assessments of the leadership potential of the bosses were significantly related to their company's profits. What's more, the instant judgements were more accurate than those of senior managers rating the bosses they actually worked for.

21

ACKNOWLEDGEMENTS

Special thanks to Lucy Warburton at Quarto for commissioning the book, and to Stuart Tolley for the design. Thank you to Nick Sunderland, for his dissection of the word 'ESPELIDES' in 'First Thoughts'. Thanks to Sgnuj. An additional thank you to Roelof Bakker, Alfonso Batalla, Martin Crawley, Neil Robinson, Richard Scarborough.

Michael Atavar is an artist and author.
He has written four books on creativity –
*How to Be an Artist, 12 Rules of Creativity,
Everyone Is Creative* and *How to Have
Creative Ideas in 24 Steps – Better Magic*.
He also designed (with Miles Hanson)
a set of creative cards *'210CARDS'*.

He works 1-2-1, runs workshops and
gives talks about the impact of creativity
on individuals and organisations.
www.creativepractice.com